PORCELAIN MARKS OF THE WORLD

PORCELAIN MARKS OF THE WORLD

EMANUEL POCHE

ARCO PUBLISHING COMPANY, INC.
New York

Translated by Joy Moss-Kohoutová
Graphic design by Aleš Krejča

Designed and produced by Artia for
Arco Publishing Company, Inc.
219 Park Avenue South, New York, N.Y. 10003

Library of Congress Catalog Card Number 73-92270

ISBN 0-668-03403-3
Printed in Czechoslovakia
by Polygrafia
2/10/01/01/51

PREFACE

This is intended to be a clear and practical handbook that can be used by anyone interested in porcelain. It is devoted entirely to the factory marks on the ware, and is classified on the basis of the actual appearance of such marks, whether these are objects, words or letters. The reproductions of the marks are accompanied by notes on the location of the factory, the owner or company concerned, the period in which the individual mark was used, and the technique employed in marking the items.

Marks used by modellers or decorators are not included. Such information is sometimes useful, but it would swell this book to cumbersome proportions and cut across any aim of making it a work of reference that the general reader can afford. These artists' marks—which, incidentally, have not yet been brought together in a comprehensive publication—can be gleaned from specialist literature based on the kind of marks given here, which are the most important factors in determining when and where porcelain was made. Only in a few instances, where it helps to describe the ware more precisely, have I included an artist's mark.

In general, I have put on record as many porcelain marks as I possibly could, given the size of the book. Many variants which are similar to one another and come from the same factory — such as different ways of writing the same name—had to be omitted (unless they indicated a different date of origin). On the other hand, I have included marks of English bone china, which is not strictly porcelain. For the uninitiated owner of ceramic products, it is often difficult to decide whether a piece is hard-paste or soft-paste porcelain, or even pottery; the shapes, textures and decorative techniques are often quite similar. By learning the provenance of his possessions through this handbook, the collector should be able to solve this and similar problems.

Porcelain Marks of the World is based on my personal experience — on many years of working to build up the porcelain collection of the Prague Museum of Arts and Crafts, which is one of the biggest in Central Europe. On the basis of my own findings, which agree with those of the outstanding ceramicists, I have put together a book which, hopefully, will prove an efficient guide to its subject.

Emanuel Poche

PORCELAIN MARKS OF THE WORLD

Porcelain marks are not as old as porcelain itself, but they have been used since the early medieval period. Porcelain was made from the 9th century, if not earlier, and the first great centres of production were the Chinese imperial factories in Kiangsi province (11th century); but the oldest surviving porcelain marks date only from the reign of the Ming emperor Hung Wu (1368—98). For centuries the chief marks on Chinese porcelain were imperial reign marks — appropriately enough in view of the world-wide prestige of porcelain and the absolute power of the Chinese emperor. These reign marks, generally known as *nien hao,* consist of six, or in a few cases four, characters. The characters are arranged in two columns which are always read from top to bottom, beginning with the right-hand column. The two upper right-hand characters indicate the dynasty—until 1643 the Ming, then from 1644 to 1912 the Ch'ing or Manchu dynasty. The third character signifies the family name of the ruling emperor, whose other name is given at the top of the left-hand column. The second character in this column means 'period', and the lowest means 'make' or 'made'.

Sometimes the marks are in a horizontal position, with the name of the dynasty missing; in this instance the marks must be read from right to left. The earliest marks were all inscribed by hand in cobalt under the glaze, but from the beginning of the Ch'ing dynasty there also appear imprints made with seals. These are stylized versions of the characters, being squeezed into a square-shape. However, they can be read off in the same order as other marks.

Unlike the marks later used in Europe, Chinese marks are not always reliably dated. The main reason for this was the growing foreign demand for Chinese porcelain, which was particularly noticeable from Ch'ing times. Chinese factories did not hesitate to use the marks of long dead rulers and past years on products intended chiefly for export *(ko huo),* thus endowing them with a spurious antiquity and rarity value. They even used the old forms of the characters. Spotting such frauds therefore requires long experience and great knowledge of the decorative motifs and colours used on porcelain. Only a few specialists have this, and so it is unlikely that most Chinese porcelain which passes as Ming is really original. Many items are 18th- and 19th-century imitations, including some that were even made abroad—in Japan or Europe—and then given Chinese marks.

The same situation exists with regard to Japanese marked porcelain. The Japanese, however, used various special indications that made it clear that older marks were being imitated.

In addition to the imperial marks on Chinese porcelain there are also sometimes date marks. The dates fall within a sixty year system which the Chinese used as a measure of time in the same way as Europeans use centuries. (The sixty year cycle begins with the year 2637 BC!) Since the porcelain marks do not indicate which sixty year cycle is involved, it must be deduced from the characteristics of the object itself. Where they appear at all, there are always two sixty year cycle marks next to each other.

The place name marks can be a further source of confusion. They give no concrete indication of the locality involved, and even the information they do supply is by no means unambiguous. Sometimes they really indicate the place of production, though in unspecific terms; but quite often what they name is the warehouse from which the porcelain was shipped or the merchant who sold it. There are even instances where these marks represent the buyer of the product, his address and similar details. Such inscriptions often had a kind of poetic significance that was perfectly comprehensible to contemporaries, though it is quite meaningless to us.

Equally lacking in significance now are the so-called dedication marks, representing the names of people who are unidentifiable today. More valuable are advertising marks, which recommend the product through a distinctive and exaggerated poetic terminology; this often contains features that enable the expert to date the object. Very useful, but unfortunately very rare, are the signatures of modellers and decorators. Most of their names mean nothing to modern art historians, but they too indicate a year of production which may at least be the true one. Finally, Chinese porcelain has symbolic marks such as the Eight Buddhist symbols, the Eight Precious Things, and the like.

The marks on Chinese porcelain tell us many things. They reveal, indirectly, the structure of the social system of feudal China. They reveal the complexity of Chinese culture and the Chinese spirit. And above all they reveal the great Chinese love of porcelain, and their pride in it as a creation of their own, famous throughout Asia and Europe. In Europe, from the 14th-century report by Marco Polo to the 'discovery' of its components in Saxony at the beginning of the 18th century, porcelain from China and Japan was regarded as something miraculous and very precious, quite on a par with the other treasures of palaces, churches and the mansions of the wealthy.

The marks used by the other major producer of porcelain in eastern Asia—Japan—are of a different nature. As early as the beginning of the 16th century the Japanese discovered that the secret of making porcelain lay in the use of china clay as the main element, a fact that remained unknown to Europeans for another two hundred years. As well as utilizing the knowledge, experience and ingenuity of Chinese porcelain makers, the Japanese adopted the Chinese custom of marking, mostly in Chinese characters, the time and place of origin and even the maker. However, the Japanese marks are more straightforwardly informative than their Chinese counterparts, being laden with none of the allegories and obfuscations dear to the Chinese. In 645 AD the Japanese took over the *nien hao* system of reign marks (called *nengo* in Japanese), but with a different time span. Porcelain products are dated within the framework of these periods, but in view of the fact that until 1873 the Japanese did not use the Gregorian calendar, deciphering these dates is difficult and requires special tables. Furthermore the Japanese too employed the sixty year cycle, but also without properly marking the sequence of the individual periods. (They even imitated the Chinese in dating the cycles back to 2637 BC.) Within each cycle they usually list the individual years, and in view of the scope of this volume it is impossible to discuss these marks in detail. We shall therefore note only those marks that have a concrete content, in other words those that give the place of manufacture (or possibly the maker) and clearly date the product. The Japanese laid much greater stress on such data than the Chinese did. In Japan there was no imperial monopoly, so that there were far more opportunities for business enterprise. Though the marks often carry reminders of 'Great Japan', Japanese porcelain is represented by workshops scattered over almost all the provinces of the empire. The most important were the provinces of Hizen, Kaga and Yamashiro, where the centres of production were the towns of Arita, Kutani and Kyoto, whose porcelain factories created a distinctive style. Their most productive period was the 18th and 19th centuries, when great quantities of porcelain were being exported to Europe. The temptations of the export market often led to the production of pieces that looked older than they really were, and to the imitation of the style in which famous decorators of the past worked.

Japanese porcelain is outstanding for its contrasts of colour. On the one hand there is variety of colours and gilding used to create elaborate painted floral decoration; on the other hand there is the restrained drawing of bamboo shoots and tender leaves. The Japanese strove for a more immediate optical impact than is found in Chinese porcelain, where the aesthetic values are more subtle. The Japanese showed more ingenuity in producing effective decoration, and also made their own technological contribution (cloisonné enamel).

In Europe the marking of porcelain began almost as soon as it was realized that china clay (kaolin) was the main ingredient needed to make true porcelain. This occurred in Saxony at the beginning of the 18th century. However, Europeans had been experimenting for at least a century and a half, and in Italy and France had succeeded in producing versions of soft-paste porcelain. The Medici porcelain of Florence, Saint Cloud ware and other early products were marked, though the object was to record the achievement of the makers rather than to guarantee the authenticity of the objects marked and distinguish them from the wares of competitors.

These motives became important only when Johann Friedrich Böttger, an alchemist in the service of Augustus the Strong, elector of Saxony, discovered how to make hard-paste or true porcelain. The elector hoped to make its manufacture at Meissen, just outside Dresden, a Saxon monopoly, while rulers of neighbouring countries naturally attempted to follow the Saxon example. The first marks used at Meissen were the letters and numbers put on the reverse of each object from 1721; but these were more or less for purposes of registration. Various geometrical marks, incised and painted, were also used, in this case to indicate different types of Oriental porcelain which, for instance, decorated Augustus's Japanese Palace in Dresden.

Böttger's white porcelain was not marked at first; only later did the letters W. R. appear on it. Around 1721—2 the marking of Meissen porcelain became general practice; the mark used was the so-called Caduceus, which at first resembled Mercury's or Aesculapius' staff. It was used for about ten years, particularly on pieces intended for export. In 1723 another factory mark was introduced, Kite or 'Drachenmarke'.

Apart from these marks, which gave no specific indication of provenance, a mark giving the place of origin was introduced in 1722: the letters M.P.M. (Meissner Porzellanmanufaktur) or K.P.M. (Königliche Porzellanmanufaktur), which were however employed only on pots and sugar basins. A year later a mark was adopted which is used to this day and has become world famous: crossed swords (taken from the coat of arms of Saxony), at first combined with the mark K.P.M. From 1724 the crossed swords mark was used on its own (though it was not officially introduced until 1731), and to this day it is the exclusive mark of Meissen production. At the outset the crossed swords were impressed, but later they were painted in cobalt blue under the glaze, as they have been ever since. Over the centuries the actual drawing of this mark has undergone several alterations. Other marks were also sometimes added, and these often gave their names to the periods in question. Thus during the dot period a dot was placed between the cross-guards of the swords; the term applies to the period 1763—80 although, as Rückert has pointed out, the dot occasionally appeared as early as the 1730's. The same is true of the star between the sword hilts, which gave its name to the star period, when the factory was managed by Count Camillo Marcolini (1774—1814); in this period there were still other additional marks, from which it is possible to deduce the names of the heads of the painting workshop. From the 1760's the quality of inferior items was indicated by incised lines crossing the mark once, twice or three times over or under the swords. Porcelain ordered for the king and his court between 1723 and 1736 carried the monogram AR (Augustus Rex). Special marks were also made on porcelain manufactured for the Saxon court in Dresden and in Warsaw (Augustus being king of Poland as well as elector of Saxony).

Apart from factory marks, some products of the 1730's carried impressed marks made by the modeller; then, in 1740, modellers' marks were replaced by numerals. Finally, the numbering of models, carried out retrospectively in 1749 when the manufacture was directed by J. J. Kändler, added to the difficulty of deciphering Meissen markings. Such was the productivity of Meissen that by 1764 no less than 3051 models had been registered.

The crossed swords mark is the oldest European porcelain mark that is still in use. It symbolizes an output which, in the 18th century, and particularly thanks to J.J. Kändler, achieved the status of high art. As such it had a tremendous influence on contemporary culture, of which it gives us an especially vivid picture.

It is interesting that Meissen's closest competitor, the factory in imperial Vienna, left its products unmarked for nearly three decades. This can hardly be explained by the involvement of private enterprise in the person of Claudius Innocentius du Paquier, since the Berlin entrepreneur Wegely marked his ware with his own monogram. Apparently du Paquier did not mark ware from his factory for the simple reason that it was not yet custom in 1718, when he started production.

Viennese porcelain began to be marked only when the factory was bought by the state in 1744. The mark chosen was the emblem of the duchy of Austria, a heraldic shield with a beam across it. Its shape gave rise to the erroneous belief that it was intended to represent a beehive. The Viennese imperial porcelain factory employed this mark, which was first impressed, then painted, and later still impressed again, for more than a hundred years, until the factory closed in 1864.

As well as the factory mark, Vienna porcelain carried complicated subsidiary markings which provided information about the maker and the date of production. In the 18th century porcelain figures carried modellers' marks in the form of various impressed letters; in the 19th century the presence of painted numerals provided information about several generations of painters of all genres—figure painters and decorative painters, and painters of landscapes and still-lifes. The factory also indicated the year of production with impressed numbers; and the practice was copied by several other porcelain factories in the Austro-Hungarian Empire, including the Czech factories at Slavkov and Klášterec nad Ohří.

With the expansion of porcelain production in the German states and throughout Europe in the later 18th century, marking systems became the rule. Royal and aristocratic entrepreneurs, stimulated by the achievements of the factories at Meissen, Vienna and Venice, vied with one another in setting up their own concerns, and in the process developed a number of systems of marking porcelain. The two Ls monogram of Louis XV appeared on Sèvres porcelain, and in the 18th and 19th centuries the monograms of various monarchs, shown with a crown, were commonly seen. But an even more popular way of marking porcelain in the 19th century was to use a symbolic motif. The symbol of the state or ruler was shown through some heraldic device (a coat of arms, or certain elements of one, or else the ruler's insignia), often followed by a symbol representing the place of production. In addition to the heraldic marks already mentioned, there are those of St Petersburg, Nymphenburg and Herend, and of Italian and Spanish porcelain. In the second category it is possible to include the silhouette of the dome of Florence Cathedral on Medici porcelain, as well as the motif of the sea on Copenhagen porcelain; and there are a good many others.

With the further expansion of porcelain production in the 19th century, the period of the industrial revolution, hundreds and hundreds of new porcelain factories sprang up. The resulting fierce competition, haste and mechanization of production did not encourage painstaking differentiation between marks by means of symbols. It became the practice for a firm to follow the English example and simply give its name, either in full or in abbreviated form, which sufficiently indicated the locality and/or ownership of the company. The symbol, where it was still used, became at best a minor decorative motif. There were fewer hand-written marks, and with the introduction of copperplate printing on porcelain (also based on the English model) printed marks made with a stamp became commonplace. But the desire for profit or the need to survive sometimes came into conflict with the principle of correct marking. In such cases, marks were altered so as to resemble the symbols or monograms of the factories manufacturing the best wares. This tendency had been in evidence from the earliest days of European porcelain; at Meissen, for example, Böttger's products had been inscribed with Oriental, usually Chinese, characters and symbols. Similarly, 18th-century English businessmen at Derby, Worcester and Caughley did not hesitate to use quasi-Oriental marks, tacitly claiming that their ware was comparable in quality to Oriental porcelain. These earlier practices concealed no fraudulent intentions; they were, rather, an expression of admiration and respect for centuries of Oriental tradition, as well as representing an attempt to exploit its popularity. In the 19th century, practices of this sort were less innocent in intention. Many marks were intended to create the impression that the ware had been produced at one of the great European centres. The Meissen mark was imitated in England (at Chelsea, Derby, Worcester and Bristol), in Belgium (at Tournai), in Holland (at Weesp), and in Germany itself at such factories as Rauenstein, Limbach, Nymphenburg, Volkstedt and Wallendorf. In Bohemia the Loket and Dubí factories imitated Meissen; and as far away as Russia the Englishman Francis Gardner did the same at Verbilki. Sèvres porcelain, with its world-wide reputation, also proved a magnet for imitators, who copied the famous intertwined Ls; among the imitators were the factories at Valenciennes, Limoges and Foëcy in France, Derby and Worcester in England, and several lesser known porcelain factories in Germany. The mark of the imperial factory in Vienna was imitated too, but not so blatantly as the Sèvres and Meissen marks—probably because the Viennese factory was gradually declining in importance. But a modern firm that has complicated the identification of Viennese porcelain is the Vienna-Augarten, which since 1922 has been manufacturing ware in modern styles, but has also produced historicizing porcelain, including tableware with subjects taken from the Neo-Classical Sorgenthal period.

The leading factories naturally did their best to protect themselves against imitation of their marks, even if only a general similarity was involved. The effectiveness of such imitations was thus often ephemeral. Yet such forgeries and imitations have managed to deceive experienced collectors and the curators of museum collections, and it has therefore become necessary to devote increased attention to marks and to assess them in the context of the overall character of the object concerned. In trying to discover where and when it was made, the basic criterion is always the nature of the material used. In certain cases this can be an absolutely decisive consideration. For example, some porcelain factories have disposed of—still dispose of—original models from which new casts can be taken again and again. Superficially there may be no way of telling whether an object is two years or two hundred years old. This is most notoriously true of Meissen, but it also applies to Höchst, whose models were taken over by the factory at Damm, which even used the same mark as Höchst. This, however, was merely an episode around 1800, whereas Meissen 'Rococo porcelain' is manufactured to this day with 18th-century lavishness and superb technique. The Berlin factory too has made new casts from 18th-century models. However, since the 19th century Berlin has used different marks for its products, including casts made from 18th-century models; so there is no difficulty in distinguishing between the old and the new.

Where the mark is the same, detailed examination will generally show up the differences. The body of a modern cast is usually smooth and unbroken; for instance the bases of the figures are not cracked. The glaze is brilliant and shiny, and the tones of the colours often differ from those of the 18th-century palette. This is particularly true of the countless idyllic Rococo-like figures and groups which, thanks to their decorative charm, remain enormously popular with the public at large.

Modern copies of tableware are even easier to spot. Copyists make all sorts of mistakes as to both the shape of the ware—overemphasizing its 'period' features—and its painted decoration. Modern decorators are never as successful as their 18th- and early 19th-century predecessors in creating Rococo and Neo-Classical subjects such as flowers, landscapes, figures and scenes. In particular, they find it impossible to simulate the brushwork of the old painters. Even in China and Japan, where imitating ancient models was a traditional occupation (pursued with such success by the 18th century that the results were often indistinguishable from the originals), the craft declined in the 19th century. Here too the copy is always given away by the brushstrokes, the subject matter, or the composition of the materials employed.

It should be clear from all this that the authenticity of marks must always be verified. The mark must be examined with the character of the object itself in mind, and all the more so since porcelain is perhaps the only art in which historicism is still alive today. Deliberate forgeries apart, there is a continuing popular demand for pseudo-Rococo tableware and modern 'kitch' reproductions of the Empire style. Porcelain lends itself perfectly to Rococo and Neo-Classicism, with the result that these have become the accepted styles for any artistic work in the medium. Only modern utility porcelain, and some decorative porcelain produced by outstanding artists at such factories as Sèvres, Copenhagen, Ludwigsburg and Meissen, have broken with tradition and struck any kind of modern note.

And this may change in the future. For although this once precious material has become a daily commonplace, its qualities are such that it is unlikely ever to be replaced by some modern synthetic material.

MARKS

NOTE ON THE CLASSIFICATION OF MARKS

The marks in this book are grouped according to their subject matter. This seemed the arrangement best suited to the practical needs of readers, for whom the factory mark of an object is the chief and most reliable indication of when, where and by whom it was made. One group here consists of marks whose main motifs are pictorial symbols, in another and much larger group the main features are place names, or the names or monograms of the producers. However, it is a very difficult matter to classify all the marks so unambiguously since some of them are composed of more than one symbol. In such cases the author could only decide for himself to which group a particular mark belonged. For this reason, when readers are investigating a mark they should check up on all the motifs to be found on it.

The sequence of groups is as follows: the sun 1—7; the moon 8—19; the stars 20—30; water 31—3; flora 34—79; man and parts of his body 80—87; fauna 88—122; insignia and heraldic devices 123—234; emblems 235—6; 'Zachenbalken' 237—8; arms 239—55; implements, instruments and machines 256—313; buildings 314—28; symbols and geometric motifs 329—59; Roman alphabet marks 360—1738; Cyrillic alphabet marks 1739—1801; Oriental marks 1802—2031; European imitations of Oriental marks 2032—2061.

LIST OF ABBREVIATIONS

B	Belgium
DK	Denmark
DDR	German Democratic Republic
D	German Federal Republic
GB	Great Britain
F	France
N	Netherlands
IRL	Ireland
I	Italy
J	Japan
YU	Yugoslavia
L	Luxembourg
PL	Poland
P	Portugal
R	Rumania
SU	USSR
S	Sweden
CH	Switzerland
E	Spain
CS	Czechoslovakia
H	Hungary

1

SAINT CLOUD
Royal Porcelain Factory
1693—1722 / *blue*

2

SAINT CLOUD
Royal Porcelain Factory
1693—1722 / *blue*

3

SAINT CLOUD
Royal Porcelain Factory
1693—1722 / *blue*

4

VOLKSTEDT-RUDOLSTADT
H. Greiner
1808—1870 / *blue*

5

LICHTE
Heubach Bros
19th cent. / *printed*

6

TURN (Trnovany)
Riessner & Kessel, "Amphora"
from 1892 / *printed*

7

SCHIRNDING
Porzellanfabrik
from 1902 / *printed*

8

BOW
W. Duesbury
1762—1776 / *blue*

9

WORCESTER
Dr Wall
1751—1783 / *blue*

10

WORCESTER
Dr Wall
1751—1783 / *red*

11

WORCESTER
Dr Wall
1751—1783 / *red*

12

LOWESTOFT
imitations of Worcester
2nd half of 18th cent. / *blue*

13
14

CAUGHLEY
T. Turner
1772—1799 / *blue*

15
16

CAUGHLEY
T. Turner
1772—1799 / *blue*

17

PINXTON
W. Billingsley
1796—1813 / *red*

18

COPENHAGEN
Royal Porcelain Factory
19th cent. / *impressed*

19

OESLAU
W. Goebel
from 1879 / *printed*

20

DOCCIA
L. Ginori
1770—1790 / *red*

21

DOCCIA
C. L. Ginori
late 18th—early 19th cent.
blue, red, gold

22
23
24

DOCCIA
C. L. Ginori
late 18th —early 19th cent. / *blue*

25
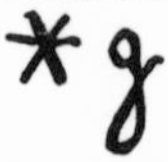
DOCCIA
Ginori
late 19th cent. / *impressed*

26
27

LE NOVE
E. P. Antonibon
from 1763 / *red, gold*
/ *blue, red, gold*

28

LONGTON
Paragon China Ltd.
from 1919 / *printed*

29

NOVGOROD
Kuznetsov
1st half of 19th cent. / *blue*

30

TOMASZOW
M. Mezer
1806—1810 / *printed*

31

COPENHAGEN
Royal Porcelain Factory
1830—1845 / *blue*

32

COPENHAGEN
Royal Porcelain Factory
1830—1845 / *blue*

33

COPENHAGEN
Royal Porcelain Factory
1830—1845 / *blue*

34

SCHLAGGENWALD (Slavkov)
Haas & Czjizek
1888—1906 / *printed*

35

SCHLAGGENWALD (Slavkov)
Haas & Czjizek
20th cent. / *printed*

36

SCHLAGGENWALD (Slavkov)
Haas & Czjizek
1888—1896 / *printed*

37

CHODAU (Chodov)
Haas & Czjizek
from 1905 / *printed*

38

WALDENBURG (Walbrzych)
Krister Porzellanmanufaktur
1831 —1943 / *blue*

39

REHAU
Zeh, Scherzer & Co.
from 1880 / *printed*

40

CAPODIMONTE
Royal Porcelain Factory
1743—1759 / *impressed*

41

PARIS, PONT AUX CHOUX
"Mignon"
1777—1784 / *blue*

42

SAINT CLOUD
Royal Porcelain Factory
1696 / *incised*

43
44

PARIS, PONT AUX CHOUX
"Mignon"
1777—1784 / *blue*

45
46

CAPODIMONTE
Royal Porcelain Factory
1743—1759 / *blue*

47

BUEN RETIRO
Royal Porcelain Factory
1760—1803 / *blue*

48

CAPODIMONTE
Royal Porcelain Factory
1743—1759 / *blue*

49
50
51

BUEN RETIRO
Royal Porcelain Factory
1760—1803 / *blue*

52

BUEN RETIRO
Royal Porcelain Factory
1760—1803 / *blue*

53

CHELSEA
N. Sprimont & C. Gouyn
1745—1749 / *blue*

54

LIMBACH
G. Greiner
after 1787 / *red, green, gold, black*

55
56

KLOSTER VEILSDORF
G. Greiner
1797—1822 / *blue*

57

ORLÉANS
Manufacture Royale
after 1753(?) or
after 1766 / *blue*

58

PARIS, RUE DE LA ROQUETTE
Souroux
after 1773 / *blue, red*

59

CHARLOTTENBRUNN
(Zofiówka)
J. Schachtel
after 1859 / *printed*

60

ALT-ROHLAU (Stará Role)
M. Zdekauer
after 1881 / *printed*

61

NIEDERSALZBRUNN
(Szczawienko)
H. Ohme
after 1882 / *printed*

62

WUNSIEDEL
Retsch & Co.
after 1885 / *printed*

63

WUNSIEDEL
Retsch & Co.
after 1885 / *printed*

64

COALPORT
J. Rose
after 1796 / *printed*

65

MERKELSGRÜN (Merklín)
1881—1918 / *printed*

66

MARKTREDWITZ
Jaeger & Co.
after 1872 / *printed*

67

SCHAALA
H. Voigt
after 1872 / *printed*

68

POTSCHAPPEL
C. Thieme
after 1872 / *printed*

69

LICHTE
Heubach Bros
after 1820 / *blue*

70

PLAUE
C. G. Schierholz & Sohn
after 1817 / *blue*

71

PLAUE
C. G. Schierholz & Sohn
after 1817 / *printed*

72

PLAUE
C. G. Schierholz & Sohn
after 1817 / *printed*

73

GROSSBREITENBACH
G. Greiner
after 1783 / *blue*

74

LIMBACH
G. Greiner
after 1787 / *blue*

75

ILMENAU
G. Greiner
1787—1792 / *blue*

76

LIMBACH
Porcelain Factory
middle of 19th cent.
printed

77

GROSSBREITENBACH
H. Bühl & Söhne
19th cent. / *printed*

78

DUX (Duchcov)
E. Eichler
after 1860 / *printed*

79

GEHREN
J. Günthersfeld & Co.
after 1884 / *printed*

80

MILAN
San Cristoforo
after 1945 / *printed*

81

VIENNA, WILHELMSBURG
Oest. Keramik A. G.
1883—1945 / *printed*

82

OHRDRUF
Baehr & Proeschild
after 1871 / *printed*

83

ELBOGEN (Loket)
R. & F. Haidinger
1815—1833 / *blue*

84

ELBOGEN (Loket)
R. & F. Haidinger
1833—1860 / *impressed*

85

ELBOGEN (Loket)
Springer & Co.
c. 1900 / *blue*

86

ELBOGEN (Loket)
"Epiag"
1938—1945 / *blue*

87

PÖSSNECK
Conta & Böhme
after 1790 / *blue*

88

KASSEL
Friedrich II of Hesse-Kassel
1766—1788 / *blue*

89

FRANKENTHAL
J. A. Hannong
1756—1759 / *blue*

90

MARKTSCHWABEN
Keramische Fabrik
19th cent. / *printed*

91

HEREND
Porcelain Factory
1897 / *printed*

92

TETTAU
G. C. Greiner
after 1885 / *gold*

93

SWINTON
Royal Rockingham Works
1820—1842 / *printed*

94

FÜRSTENBERG
Fürstliche Porzellanmanufactur
1770—1814 / *impressed*

95

UNTERWEISSBACH
Mann & Porzelius A. G.
19th cent. / *printed*

96

KLÖSTERLE (Klášterec)
M. Weber
1796—1803 / *red, black*

97
98

KLÖSTERLE (Klášterec)
M. Weber
1804—1830 / *blue, various colours*

99

LUDWIGSBURG
Carl Eugen of Württemberg
1759—1806 / *blue*

100

LUDWIGSBURG
Carl Eugen of Württemberg
1759—1806 / *blue*

101

LUDWIGSBURG
Carl Eugen of Württemberg
1759—1806 / *blue*

102

KATZHÜTTE
Hertwig & Co.
19th cent. until 1945 / *impressed*

103
104

HAGUE
A. & J. F. Lynker
1776—1790 / *blue*

105

HAGUE
A. & J. F. Lynker
1776—1790 / *blue*

106

HAGUE
A. & J. F. Lynker
1776—1790 / *blue*

107

SUHL
E. Schlegelmilch
after 1861 / *printed*

108

VIENNA, WILHELMSBURG
Oest. Keramik A. G.
1883—1945 / *printed*

109

FENTON
E. Brain & Co.
after 1900 / *printed*

110

BARCELONA
Manufacturas Cerámicas
after 1921 / *printed*

111

MARKTREDWITZ
Jaeger & Co.
after 1872 / *printed*

112

ANSBACH
Markgräfliche Porzellan-manufaktur
1758—1790 / *blue*

113

ANSBACH
Markgräfliche Porzellan-manufaktur
1758—1790 / *blue*

114
115

NYON
J. Dortu & F. Müller
1781—1813 / *blue*

116

KÖPPELSDORF
J. Hering & Sohn
after 1893 / *printed*

117

LILLE
Leperre-Durot
1784—1817 / *red*

118

LILLE
Leperre-Durot
1784—1817 / *red*

119

MITTERTEICH
M. Emanuel & Co.
after 1900 / *printed*

120

OESLAU
W. Goebel
after 1879 / *printed*

121

EICHWALD (Dubí)
Bloch & Co.
after 1871 / *blue*

122

POSTSCHAPPEL
C. Thieme
after 1872 / *blue*

123

MARIEBERG
P. Berthevin
1777—1778 / *red, blue*

124

MARIEBERG
P. Berthevin
1777—1778 / *red, blue*

125

RÖRSTRAND
B. R. Geyer
beginning of 19th cent. / *blue gold*

126

EICHWALD (Dubí)
Bloch & Co.
after 1871 / *blue*

127

LANGEWIESEN
O. Schlegelmilch
after 1872 / *blue*

128

HILDESHEIM
after 1760 / *blue*

129 

BUEN RETIRO
Charles III of Spain
after 1759 / *blue*

---

130 

DERBY
Crown Porcelain Co.
1877—1889 / *printed*

---

131 

DERBY
Crown Porcelain Co.
after 1890 / *printed*

---

132 

DERBY
Crown Porcelain Co.
1784—1811 / *gold*

---

133 

BOCK-WALLENDORF
Fasold & Stauch
after 1903 / *printed*

---

134 

WORCESTER
Royal Worcester Porcelain Co.
from 1862 / *printed*

---

135 

FENTON
Crown Staffordshire China
after 1801 / *printed*

---

136 

FISCHERN (Rybáře)
C. Knoll
beginning of 20th cent. / *printed*

137 

WALDENBURG (Walbrzych)
C. Tielsch
2nd half of 19th cent. / *blue*

---

138 

PIRKENHAMMER (Březová)
after 1890 until 1938 / *red, printed*

---

139 

COPENHAGEN
Royal Porcelain Factory
1905 / *gold*

---

140 

COPENHAGEN
Royal Porcelain Factory
1905 / *gold*

---

141 

COPENHAGEN
Royal Porcelain Factory
from 1929 / *gold*

---

142 

KAHLA
Porcelain Factory
after 1844 / *printed*

---

143 

ELLWANGEN
A. F. Prahl's widow
c. 1760 / *blue*

---

144 

ELLWANGEN
A. F. Prahl's widow
c. 1760 / *blue*

145

HELSINKI
Arabia A/B
1874—1917 / *printed*

146

HEREND
Porcelain Factory
c. 1850 / *blue*

147

HEREND
Porcelain Factory
1900—1934 / *blue*

148

HEREND
Porcelain Factory
1891—1897 / *blue*

149

FRYAZINO
Barmin Bros
1820—1850 / *blue*

150

HOHENBERG
C. M. Hutschenreuther
1865 / *printed*

151

BADEN-BADEN
Z. Pfalzer
1771—1778 / *blue*

152

SAARGEMÜND
Utzschneider & Co.
19th cent. / *printed*

153

SAARGEMÜND
Utzschneider & Co.
19th cent. / *printed*

154

TURN (Trnovany)
E. Wahliss, "Alexandra-Porcelain-Works"
after 1894 / *printed*

155
156

TIRSCHENREUTH
Porzellanfabrik
2nd half of 19th cent. / *printed*

157

TURN (Trnovany)
E. Wahliss, "Alexandra-Porcelain-Works"
after 1894 / *printed*

158

HELSINKI
Arabia A/B
after 1874 / *printed*

159
160

REHAU
Zeh, Scherzer & Co.
c. 1900 / *printed*

161

ANSBACH
Markgräfliche Porzellanmanufaktur
last quarter of 18th cent.
impressed

162

ANSBACH
Markgräfliche Porzellanmanufaktur
c. 1765 and 19th cent. / *blue*

163

ANSBACH
Markgräfliche Porzellanmanufaktur
c. 1765 and 19th cent. / *blue*

164

VIENNA
Staatsmanufaktur
2nd half of 18th cent. / *blue*

165

VIENNA
Staatsmanufaktur
1744—1749 / *incised*

166

VIENNA
Staatsmanufaktur
1749—1820 / *blue*

167

VIENNA
Staatsmanufaktur
1744—1749 / *impressed*

168

VIENNA
Staatsmanufaktur
1820—1827 / *blue*

169

VIENNA
Staatsmanufaktur
1760—1770 / *blue*

170
171

NYMPHENBURG
Kurfürstliche Porzellanmanufaktur
1755—1765 / *impressed*

172

NYMPHENBURG
Kurfürstliche Porzellanmanufaktur
1810—1850 / *impressed*

173

NYMPHENBURG
Kurfürstliche Porzellanmanufaktur
1780—1790 / *impressed*

174

NYMPHENBURG
Kurfürstliche Porzellanmanufaktur
1850—1862 / *impressed*

175
176

FRANKENTHAL
P. Hannong
1755—1759 / *blue*

177

BLANKENHAIN
C. & A. Carstens
19th cent. / *blue*

178

PIRKENHAMMER (Březová)
Fischer & Mieg
after 1887—1890 / *gold*

179
180
181

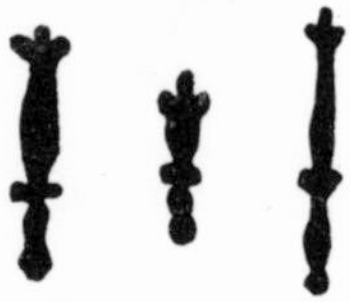

BERLIN
Königliche Porzellanmanufaktur
1763—1780 / *blue*

182
183

BERLIN
Königliche Porzellanmanufaktur
1780—1880 / *blue*

184

BERLIN
Königliche Porzellanmanufaktur
1875—1944 / *blue*

185

BERLIN
Königliche Porzellanmanufaktur
1847—1849 / *printed*

186

BERLIN
Königliche Porzellanmanufaktur
1849—1870 / *printed*

187

PASSAU
Dressel, Kister & Co.
2nd half of 19th cent. / *blue*

188

MEISSEN
Böttger stoneware
1707—1720 / *impressed*

189

MEISSEN
J. F. Böttger
1710—1720 / *blue*

190

MEISSEN
Königliche Porzellanmanufaktur
1725—1730 / *blue*

191

MEISSEN
Königliche Porzellanmanufaktur
1730 / *blue*

192

MEISSEN
Königliche Porzellanmanufaktur
1731 / *blue*

193

MEISSEN
Königliche Porzellanmanufaktur
1723—1724 / *blue*

194
195

MEISSEN
Königliche Porzellanmanufaktur
1725—1730 / *blue*

196

MEISSEN
Königliche Porzellanmanufaktur
1725—1730 / *blue*

197 

MEISSEN
Königliche Porzellanmanufaktur
1730—1735 / *blue*

198 

MEISSEN
Königliche Porzellanmanufaktur
1730—1740 / *blue*

199 

MEISSEN
Königliche Porzellanmanufaktur
after 1750 / *blue*

200 

MEISSEN
Königliche Porzellanmanufaktur
1730—1740 / *blue*

201 

MEISSEN
Königliche Porzellanmanufaktur
c. 1765 / *blue*

202
203

MEISSEN
Königliche Porzellanmanufaktur
after 1763 / *blue*

204
205

MEISSEN
Königliche Porzellanmanufaktur
after 1774 / *blue*

206 

MEISSEN
Königliche Porzellanmanufaktur
1772 and after 1774 / *blue*

207 

MEISSEN
Königliche Porzellanmanufaktur
1774—1830 / *impressed*

208

MEISSEN
Königliche Porzellanmanufaktur
beginning of 19th cent. / *blue*

209

MEISSEN
Königliche Porzellanmanufaktur
after 1723, with mark of Master
Kretschner added / *blue*

210

MEISSEN
Königliche Porzellanmanufaktur
1st half of 18th cent., with mark
of Master Moebius / *blue*

211

MEISSEN
Königliche Porzellanmanufaktur
after 1766, medium quality
blue

212

MEISSEN
Königliche Porzellanmanufaktur
after 1766, medium quality,
unpainted / *blue*

213

MEISSEN
Königliche Porzellanmanufaktur
after 1766, medium quality,
painted / *blue*

214

MEISSEN
Königliche Porzellanmanufaktur
after 1766, discarded,
painted / *blue*

215

MEISSEN
Königliche Porzellanmanufaktur
after 1766, discarded,
unpainted / *blue*

216

MEISSEN
Königliche Porzellanmanufaktur
after 1766, second quality,
painted / *blue*

217

MEISSEN
Königliche Porzellanmanufaktur
after 1766, third quality / *blue*

218

MEISSEN
Königliche Porzellanmanufaktur
after 1766, discarded / *blue*

219

MEISSEN
Königliche Hofconditorei
Warschau
1763—1806 / *black, red*

220

MEISSEN
Königliche Porzellanmanufaktur
after 1724, with a number
indicating the service / *blue*

221

MEISSEN
Königliche Porzellanmanufaktur
modellers' marks, 18th cent.
blue
Georg Kittel
Peter Geithner
Gottfried Lohse
Johann Christoph Krumbholtz
Johann Donner
Johann Kittel
Christoph Busch
Johann Meisel
Georg Michel
Johann Michal Schuhmann

222

VOLKSTEDT-RUDOLSTADT
C. Nonne
after 1788—1799 / *blue*

223

LOWESTOFT
imitation of Meissen mark
18th cent. / *blue*

224

CHELSEA
imitations of Meissen
18th cent. / *blue, gold*

225

WEESP
Count Gronsveldt-Diepenbroek
1759—1771 / *blue*

226

WEESP
Count Gronsveldt-Diepenbroek
1759—1771 / *blue*

227

BRISTOL
R. Champion
end of 18th cent. / *blue, incised*

228

BRISTOL
R. Champion
end of 18th cent. / *blue, incised*

229

BRISTOL
R. Champion
end of 18th cent. / *blue, incised*

230

BRISTOL
R. Champion
end of 18th cent. / *blue, incised*

231

BRISTOL
R. Champion
1773—1781 / *blue, incised*

232

WORCESTER
Dr Wall
1751 —1783 / *blue*

233

DERBY
imitations of Meissen
middle of 18th cent. / *blue*

234

TOURNAI
F. J. Peterinck
1763—1800 / *blue, gold*

235

KÖPPELSDORF
J. Hering & Sohn
c. 1893 / *printed*

236

FREIWALDAU (Gozdnica)
H. Schmidt
2nd half of 19th cent. / *printed*

237

VINCENNES
Séguin factory, coat of arms of the duke of Chartres
after 1777—1788 / *blue*

238

ORLÉANS
Manufacture Royale de porcelayne d'Orléans
1767—1806 / *blue*

239

PARIS, RUE DE LA ROQUETTE
J. V. Dubois
after 1774 / *blue*

240

EISENBERG
Porzellanfabrik Kalk G. m. b. H.
after 1900 / *blue*

241

MITTERTEICH
M. Emanuel & Co.
after 1900 / *printed*

242

BOW
Weatherby & Crowther
c. 1750 / *blue*

243

WORCESTER
Wall period
1751—1783 / *blue*

244

BOW
Weatherby & Crowther
c. 1750 / *incised*

245

GIESSHÜBEL (Kysibl)
C. Nonne & K. Roesch
1803—1811 / *blue*

246

GIESSHÜBEL (Kysibl)
B. Knaute
1815—1828 / *blue*

247
248

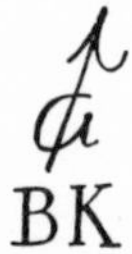

GIESSHÜBEL (Kysibl)
B. Knaute
1828—1830 / *blue*

249

PARIS, RUE DE LA ROQUETTE
F. Hébert
1741—1752 / *blue*

250

GRÄFENTHAL
Unger, Schneider, Hutschen-reuther & Co.
after 1861 / *blue*

251
252
253

GRÄFENTHAL
Unger, Schneider, Hutschen-reuther & Co.
after 1861 / *blue*

254

PARIS, RUE DE LA ROQUETTE
J. V. Dubois
after 1774 / *blue*

255

MITTERTEICH
M. Emanuel & Co.
after 1900 / *printed*

256

CHELSEA
Triangle period (Sprimont-Gouyn)
1745—1750 / *blue*

257
258

PARIS,
RUE FONTAINE AU ROY
L. Russinger
after 1771 / *blue*

259

PARIS,
RUE FONTAINE AU ROY
Pouyat
after 1800 / *blue*

260
261

VOLKSTEDT-RUDOLSTADT
C. Nonne
1787—1799 / *blue*

262

VOLKSTEDT-RUDOLSTADT
C. Nonne
1808—1890 / *blue*

263

VOLKSTEDT-RUDOLSTADT
C. Nonne
1808—1890 / *blue*

264
265

VOLKSTEDT-RUDOLSTADT
R. Eckert & Co.
after 1895—after 1900
printed

266

VOLKSTEDT-RUDOLSTADT
R. Eckert & Co.
after 1895—after 1900 / *printed*

267
268

PARIS, FAUBOURG SAINT DENIS
Pierre A. Hannong
1771—1776 / *blue*

269

KÖPPELSDORF-NORD
Schoenau Bros, Swaine & Co.
after 1854 / *blue*

270 271		ARNSTADT Porzellanfabrik after 1790 / *blue*
272		SCEAUX J. Jullien & S. Jacques 1763—1772 / *incised*
273 274		VENICE G. Cozzi 1766—1813 / *red, gold*
275		CHELSEA Anchor period (Sprimont-Fawkener) after 1753—1758 / *red*
276		CHELSEA Anchor period (Sprimont-Fawkener) after 1753—1758 / *blue*
277		CHELSEA Anchor period (Sprimont-Fawkener) after 1750—1753 / *red*
278		BOW W. Duesbury 1760—1766 / *red*
279 280		SCHWARZENBACH O. Schaller & Co. after 1882 / *printed*
281		BARANOVKA Mezer Bros 1804—1850 / *blue*
282		BOW W. Duesbury 1760—1776 / *red*
283		BOW W. Duesbury 1760—1776 / *blue, red*
284		BOW W. Duesbury 1760—1776 / *red*

285 
BOW
W. Duesbury
1760—1776 / *red*

286 
CHELSEA
Raised Anchor period
1750—1753 / *impressed*

287 
HÖCHST
Kurfürstliche Porzellan-
manufaktur
1758—1765 / *impressed*

288
289 
HÖCHST
Kurfürstliche Porzellan-
manufaktur
1750—1763 / *red, black, brown*
/ *blue*

290 
HÖCHST
Kurfürst Emmerich von Breiden-
bach
1765—1774 / *blue*

291 
PASSAU
imitations of Höchst
19th cent. / *blue*

292
293 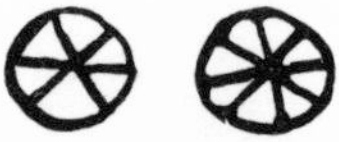
DAMM
casts from Höchst's models
1860—1888 / *blue*

294 
DAMM
casts from Höchst's models
1840—1845 / *blue*

295 
DAMM
casts from Höchst's models
1850—1860 / *blue*

296 
DAMM
casts from Höchst's models
19th cent. / *blue*

297

CHANTILLY
Prince de Condé
1726—1740 / *blue, red*

298

CHANTILLY
Prince de Condé
1740—1800 / *blue*

299

CHANTILLY
Prince de Condé
1740—1800 / *bleu*

300

ALT-ROHLAU (Stará Role)
F. Manka
from 1883 / *printed*

301

OHRDRUF
Kling & Co.
1836—1941 / *printed*

302

VIENNA
M. G. Grossbaum
1889 / *blue*

303

ALT-HALDENSLEBEN
Schmerzer & Gericke
2nd half of 19th cent. / *printed*

304

ALT-ROHLAU (Stará Role)
M. Zdekauer
after 1884 / *printed*

305

DELFT
Ary de Milde
end of 17th cent. / *impressed*

306 

LORCH
Deusch & Co.
after 1898 / *printed*

---

307 

MITTERTEICH
M. Emanuel & Co.
end of 19th cent. / *printed*

---

308 

ILMENAU
Metzler Bros & Ortloff
after 1876 / *printed*

---

309 

SCHEDEWITZ
A. Unger
20th cent. / *printed*

---

310 

STADTLENGSFELD
Porzellanfabrik A. G.
c. 1900 / *printed*

---

311 

DOCCIA
R. Ginori
18th cent. / *blue*

---

312 

KÖPPELSDORF
E. Heubach
after 1887 / *blue*

---

313 

STADTLENGSFELD
Porzellanfabrik A. G.
c. 1920 / *printed*

314

TOURNAI
F. J. Peterinck
1753—1780 / *blue, gold*

315

TOURNAI
F. J. Peterinck
1753—1780 / *gold*

316

TOURNAI
F. J. Peterinck
1753—1780 / *red, violet*

317

TOURNAI
F. J. Peterinck
1753—1780 / *gold*

318

TOURNAI
F. J. Peterinck
1752—1762 / *various colours*

319
320

TOURNAI
F. J. Peterinck
1752—1762 / *various colours*

321

TOURNAI
F. J. Peterinck
1752—1762 / *various colours*

322

PARIS, CLIGNANCOURT
P. Deruelle
after 1771—1775 / *gold*

323

PARIS, CLIGNANCOURT
P. Deruelle
after 1771—1775 / *red*

324

MANTUA,
CANETTO SULL'OGLIO
Ceramica Furga
after 1872 / *printed*

325

FLORENCE
"Medici" porcelain
1586—1620 / *blue*

326

PÉCS
Zsolnay
2nd half of 19th cent. / *blue*

327

PÉCS
Zsolnay
2nd half of 19th cent. / *printed*

328

PÉCS
Zsolnay
2nd half of 19th cent. / *printed*

329

VINOVO
G. V. Brodel, cross of the Savoy dynasty
1776—1778 / *black*

330

VINOVO
G. V. Brodel, Cross of the Savoy dynasty
1776—1778 / *blue*

331

VINOVO
G. V. Brodel
1776—1778 / *blue*

332

VINOVO
Dr V. A. Gioanetti
after 1780 until 1815 / *blue*

333

VINOVO
Porcelain factory, with the mark of the painter Carasso
before 1820 / *blue*

334

FULDA
city arms
1765—1775 / *blue*

335

BRISTOL
R. Champion
1773—1781 / *blue*

336

BRISTOL
R. Champion
1773—1781 / *blue*

337

PLYMOUTH
W. Cookworthy
after 1768—1770 / *blue or incised*

338

BOURG LA REINE
J. Jullien & S. Jacques
after 1773—1804 / *blue*

339

SITZENDORF
Voigt Bros
after 1850 / *blue*

340

BERLIN
Royal Porcelain Factory
from 1870 / *printed*

341

COPENHAGEN
F. H. Müller
after 1773 / *impressed*

342

PLAUE
C. G. Schierholz & Sohn
after 1817 / *blue*

343
344

PLAUE
C. G. Schierholz & Sohn
after 1817 / *blue*

345

SITZENDORF
Voigt Bros
after 1850 / *blue*

346

WORCESTER
Mark of a painter from the Wall period
1751—1783 / *blue*

347

MARIEBERG
H. Sten
1769—1788 / *blue*

348

BOW
W. Duesbury
1760—1776 / *blue*

349
350

KORZEC
Czartoryski-Mezer
1790—1797 / *gold*

351

CHELSEA
Triangle period
1745—1749 / *incised*

352

CHELSEA
Triangle period
1745—1749 / *printed*

353

WORCESTER
Wall period
1751—1783 / *blue*

354
355
356

WORCESTER
Wall period
1751—1783 / *blue*

357

WORCESTER
Wall period
1751—1783 / *blue*

358

WORCESTER
Wall period
1751—1783 / *blue*

359

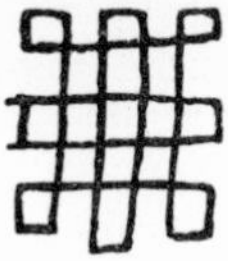

MOSCOW
Kudinov
19th cent. / *blue*

360

ALCORA
Count Aranda—P. Cloostermans
after 1786 / *brown, black*

361

ALCORA
Count Aranda—P. Cloostermans
after 1786 / *gold*

362

ALCORA
Count Aranda—P. Cloostermans
after 1786 / *incised*

363

BOW
3rd period, W. Duesbury
1760—1776 / *blue*

364

LONGTON HALL
W. Littler
1750—1760 / *blue*

365

PARIS, RUE THIROUX
A. M. Lebœuf
1776—1790 / *blue, red*

366

AICH (Doubí)
J. Möhling
1849—1860 / *impressed*

367

TURN (Trnovany)
Riessner & Kessel
after 1892 / *printed*

368

ANSBACH
Markgräfliche Porzellanmanufaktur
after 1758 / *blue*

369

ANSBACH
Markgräfliche Porzellanmanufaktur
after 1758 / *blue*

370
371
372

ANSBACH
Markgräfliche Porzellan-
manufaktur
after 1758 / *blue*

373

ANSBACH
Markgräfliche Porzellan-
manufaktur
after 1758 / *blue*

374

SITZERODE
G. H. Macheleid
middle of 18th cent. / *blue*

375

ANSBACH
Markgräfliche Porzellan-
manufaktur
c. 1765 / *blue*

376

ANSBACH
Markgräfliche Porzellan-
manufaktur
c. 1765 / *blue*

377

ANSBACH
Markgräfliche Porzellan-
manufaktur
c. 1765 / *blue*

378

ANSBACH
mark of the palace porcelain
1757—1790 / *blue*

379

ANSBACH
mark of the palace porcelain
1757—1790 / *blue*

380

ANSBACH
mark of the palace porcelain
1757—1790 / *blue*

381
382

PARIS, RUE THIROUX
Manufacture de la Reine Marie Antoinette
1776—1790 / *blue, red*

383

WEIDEN
A. Bauscher
after 1881 / *blue*

384

ELGERSBURG
E. & F. C. Arnoldi
second half of 19th cent. / *blue*

385

BAYREUTH
painter A. C. Wanderer
1727—1748 / *blue*

386

ARZBERG
C. Schumann
after 1881 / *printed*

387

PARIS, GROS CAILLOU
Advenier & Lamare
1773—1784 / *blue*

388

LONGTON
Adderley Watership
end of 18th cent. / *printed*

389

LONGTON
Adderley Watership
beginning of 19th cent.
printed

390

LONGTON
Adderley Watership
19th cent. / *printed*

391

ILMENAU
A. Fischer
1907 / *printed*

392

ILMENAU
A. Fischer
1907 / *printed*

393

VIERZON
H. Hachez & Co.
19th cent. / *printed*

394

AICH (Doubí)
J. Möhling
1849 — 1860 / *impressed*

395

BUDAU (Budov)
A. Lang
1860—1880 / *impressed*

396

LONGTON
Royal Albert Bone China
after 1844 / *printed*

397

LONGTON
Royal Albert Bone China
after 1844 / *printed*

398

LOWESTOFT
R. Allen
after 1780 / *blue*

399

LOWESTOFT
R. Allen
after 1780 / *blue*

400

LOWESTOFT
R. Allen
after 1780 / *blue*

401

ALTENBURG
19th cent. / *printed*

402

LONGTON
Alton China
after 1950 / *printed*

403

ALT-ROHLAU (Stará Role)
B. Hasslacher
1813—1824 / *impressed*

404

ALT-ROHLAU (Stará Role)
A. Nowotny
1838—1884 / *impressed*

405

ALT-ROHLAU (Stará Role)
M. Zdekauer
1884—1920 / *printed*

406

ALT-ROHLAU (Stará Role)
M. Zdekauer
after 1920 / *printed*

407
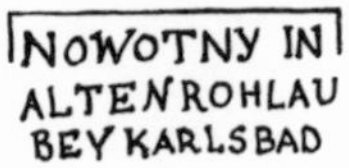

ALT-ROHLAU (Stará Role)
A. Nowotny
1838—1884 / *printed*

408

WALDENBURG (Walbrzych)
C. Tielsch
1845—1948 / *printed*

409

WALDENBURG (Walbrzych)
C. Tielsch
c. 1900 / *printed*

410

WALDENBURG (Walbrzych)
C. Tielsch
c. 1900 / *printed*

411

AICH (Doubí)
J. Möhling
c. 1860 / *impressed*

412

AICH (Doubí)
J. Möhling
before 1860 / *impressed*

413

KÖPPELSDORF-NORD
A. Marseille
after 1887 / *printed*

414

KÖPPELSDORF-NORD
A. Marseille
after 1887 / *blue*

415 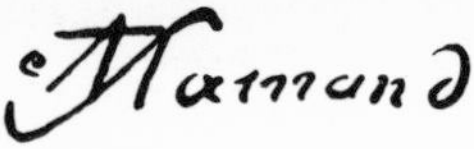

SAINT AMAND LES EAUX
Bettignies family
2nd half of 19th cent. / *blue*

416
417 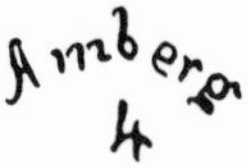

AMBERG
E. Kick
after 1850—1910 / *blue*

418 

TURN (Trnovany)
Riessner & Kessel
20th cent. / *printed*

419 

AMSTEL
Däuber period
1784—1800 / *blue*

420 

AMSTEL
G. Dommer & Co. period
1801—1809 / *black, red, gold*

421 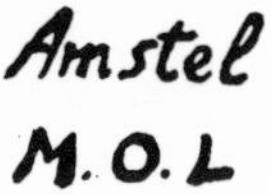

AMSTEL
Däuber period
1784—1800 / *blue*

422 

ALT-ROHLAU (Stará Role)
A. Nowotny
c. 1850 / *impressed*

423 

ALT-ROHLAU (Stará Role)
A. Nowotny
c. 1870 / *impressed*

424 

GUSTAVSBERG
1840 / *printed*

425 

SAINT CLOUD / ROUEN?
P. Chicaneau
end of 17th cent. / *blue*

426
427

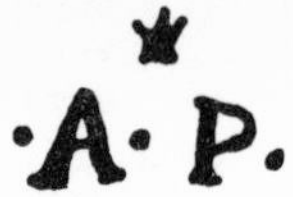

SAINT CLOUD / ROUEN?
P. Chicaneau
end of 17th cent. / *blue*

428

UNTERWEISSBACH
A. Porzelius
middle of 19th cent. / *printed*

429

MEISSEN
Augustus Rex
1723—1736 / *blue*

430

MEISSEN
Augustus Rex
1723—1736 / *blue*

431

MEISSEN
Augustus Rex
1723—1736 / *blue*

432
433

ARRAS
J. F. Boussemart & Delemer
1770—1790 / *red*

434

ARRAS
J. F. Boussemart & Delemer
1770—1790 / *blue*

435

ARRAS
Delemer
1772—1790 / *blue*

436

ARRAS
Delemer
1772—1790 / *blue*

437

MILAN
A. Richard
after 1850 / *blue*

438

COPENHAGEN
A. Mollert
18th cent. / *impressed*

439

ELBOGEN (Loket)
R. E. Haidinger
imitations of Meissen
19th cent. / *blue*

440

WEIDEN
Bauscher Bros
after 1881 / *printed*

441

KÖNIGSZELT (Jaworzyna Śląska)
A. Rosenthal & Co.
c. 1900 / *printed*

442

ALT-ROHLAU (Stará Role)
M. Zdekauer
after 1880 / *printed*

443

HELSINKI
"Arabia"
after 1948 / *printed*

444

HELSINKI
"Arabia"
after 1948 / *printed*

445 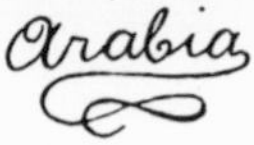

HELSINKI
"Arabia"
after 1948 / *printed*

446 

HELSINKI
"Arabia"
after 1948 / *printed*

447 

DELFT
Ary de Milde
c. 1700 / *impressed*

448 

ARZBERG
a branch of the Kahl porcelain factory
after 1890 / *printed*

449 

ARZBERG
C. M. Hutschenreuther
after 1839 / *printed*

450 

ARZBERG
C. M. Hutschenreuther
2nd half of 19th cent. / *printed*

451
452

LONGTON
Aynsley China
1st half of 19th cent. / *printed*

453 

SAINT AMAND LES EAUX
M. Bettignies
1st half of 19th cent. / *blue*

454

ALT-ROHLAU (Stará Role)
M. Zdekauer
after 1884 / *printed*

455

VIENNA, AUGARTEN
Wiener Porzellanfabrik
after 1922 / *printed*

456

VAUX
La Borde & Hocquart
1769 / *blue*

457

AICH (Doubí)
A. C. Anger
1860—1901 / *blue*

458
459

BUDAU (Budov)
F. Lang
1831—1840 / *blue*

460

BARANOVKA
M. Mezer
1804—1820 / *blue*

461

BARANOVKA
M. Mezer
1804—1820 / *red*

462

BASDORF
Schackert Bros
after 1751 / *blue*

463

BOISETTE
J. Vermonet & Fils
1778—1790 / *black, blue*

464
465
466

BOISETTE
J. Vermonet & Fils
1778—1790 / *blue*

467
468
469

WORCESTER
M. Barr
1792—1807 / *blue*

470 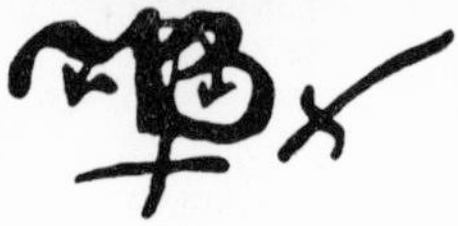

BOW
W. Duesbury
1760—1776 / *blue, red*

---

471 

BOW
T. Frye
1755—1760 / *blue*

---

472 

LASSAY
L. L. F. Comte de Lauraguais-Brancas
1763—1768 / *incised*

---

473 

BRUSSELS
J. S. Vaume
1786—1790 / *blue, red*

---

474 

BRUSSELS, SCHAERBEEK
J. S. Vaume
1786—1790 / *blue, red*

---

475 
476 

BRISTOL
W. Cookworthy
1773—1781 / *blue*

---

477 

RUDOLSTADT
E. Bohne
from 1854 / *blue*

---

478 

BARANOVKA
M. Mezer
after 1805 / *blue, gold*

---

479 
480 

BARANOVKA
M. Mezer
after 1805 / *red*

---

481 

BARANOVKA
M. Mezer
after 1805—1825 / *red*

---

482 

BARANOVKA
M. Mezer
after 1805—1825 / *blue*

483
484

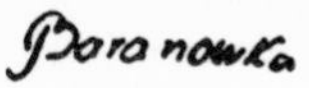

BARANOVKA
M. Mezer
after 1805—1825 / *black*

485

BARANOVKA
M. Mezer
after 1805—1825 / *black*

486

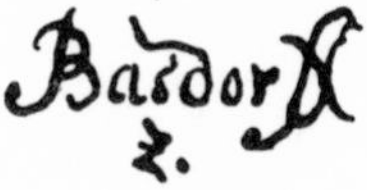

BASDORF
Schackert Bros
after 1751 / *blue*

487

PLANKENHAMMER
after 1908 / *printed*

488

WALDSASSEN
Bayreuther & Co.
after 1866 / *printed*

489

ARZBERG
C. Schumann
after 1881 / *printed*

490

WALDSASSEN
Gareis, Kühnl & Co.
after 1899 / *printed*

491

WALDSASSEN
Gareis, Kühnl & Co.
after 1899 / *printed*

492

WALDSASSEN
Gareis, Kühnl & Co.
after 1899 / *printed*

493

MARKTLEUTHEN
H. Winterling
after 1903 / *printed*

494

ERKERSREUTH
Hoffmann Bros
?0th cent. / *printed*

495

SCHWARZENBACH
J. Kronester & Co.
after 1904 / *printed*

496

MITTERTEICH
Porzellanfabrik A. G.
after 1917 / *printed*

497

MARKTREDWITZ
Jaeger & Co.
after 1872 / *printed*

498

SELB
P. Müller
1890—1912 / *printed*

499

WUNSIEDEL
Retsch & Co.
after 1885 / *printed*

500

RÖSLAU
Winterling Bros
after 1906 / *printed*

501

HOF MOSCHENDORF
O. Reinecke
after 1878 / *printed*

502

SCHWARZENBACH
O. Schaller & Co.
after 1881 / *printed*

503

SCHWARZENBACH
O. Schaller & Co.
after 1917 / *printed*

504

MARKTLEUTHEN
H. Winterling
after 1903 / *printed*

505

REHAU
Zeh, Scherzer & Co.
after 1880 / *printed*

506

REHAU
Zeh, Scherzer & Co.
after 1880 / *printed*

507

REHAU
Zeh, Scherzer & Co.
after 1880 / *printed*

508

VALOGNES—BAYEUX
M. F. Gosse
after 1849 / *gold*

509

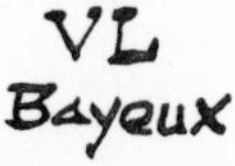

VALOGNES—BAYEUX
W. Langlois
before 1849 / *red*

510 

VALOGNES—BAYEUX
M. F. Gosse
after 1849 / *red*

---

511 

SOPHIENTHAL
Thomas & Co.
after 1948 / *printed*

---

512 

SOPHIENTHAL
Thomas & Co.
1928—1934 / *printed*

---

513 

BAYREUTH
S. P. Meyer, "Walküre"
after 1900 / *printed*

---

514 

WALDSASSEN
Bayreuther & Co.
after 1866 / *printed*

---

515 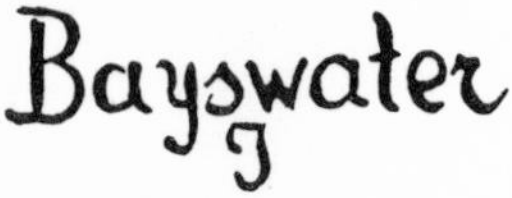

BAYSWATER
English paint-room of Chinese and European porcelain
18th—19th cent. / *printed*

---

516 

EICHWALD (Dubí)
Bloch & Co.
after 1871 / *blue*

---

517 

EICHWALD (Dubí)
Bloch & Co.
after 1871 / *blue*

518

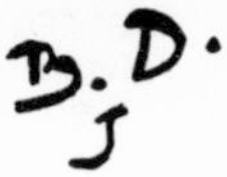

SAINT AMAND LES EAUX
J. B. Fauquez
1771—1778 / *blue*

519

LONGTON
Shore & Coggins Ltd
19th cent. / *printed*

520

LONGTON
Shore & Coggins Ltd
19th cent. / *printed*

521

BELLEEK
D. Birnay
after 1863 / *printed*

522

MAGDEBURG-BUCKAU
Buckauer Porzellanmanufaktur
after 1832 / *blue*

523

WORCESTER
Barr, Flight & Barr
1807—1813 / *impressed*

524

WORCESTER
Barr, Flight & Barr
1807—1813 / *blue*

525

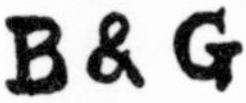

COPENHAGEN
Bing & Grøndahl
1854—1864 / *blue*

526

COPENHAGEN
Bing & Grøndahl
after 1854—1864 / *blue*

527 

COPENHAGEN
Bing & Grøndahl
after 1854—1864 / *blue*

528 

MAYERHÖFEN
Benedikt Bros
1931—1945 / *printed*

529 

LILLE
F. & B. Dorez
1720—1730 / *blue*

530 BK

GIESSHÜBEL (Kysibl)
B. Knaute
1828—1840 / *blue*

531 

REICHENSTEIN
M. Blanka
after 1831 / *blue*

532 B la R

BOURG LA REINE
J. Jullien & S. Jacques
after 1773—1804 / *impressed*

533 

DERBY
R. Bloor
1811—1849 / *printed*

534 

DERBY
R. Bloor
1811—1849 / *printed*

535 

LE NOVE
Fabbrica Antonibon
1762—1763 / *various colours, gold*

536

NIDERVILLER
J. L. de Beyerlé
1765—1770 / *red*

537

NIDERVILLER
J. L. de Beyerlé
1765—1770 / *blue*

538

NEU-ROHLAU (Nová Role)
"Bohemia"
1921 / *printed*

539

NEU-ROHLAU (Nová Role)
"Bohemia"
1921 / *printed*

540

VIENNA
G. Mladenof & Co.
after 1929 / *printed*

541

FENTON
A. Bowker
19th cent. / *printed*

542

BORDEAUX
D. Johnston
1836—1845 / *violet*

543

LONGTON
Cartwright & Edwards Ltd.
after 1858 / *printed*

544

PARIS, RUE DE CRUSSOL
C. Potter
1792—1800 / *blue*

545

BORDEAUX
Verneuilh & Alluaud
1781—1790 / *impressed*

546

BOURG LA REINE
J. Jullien & S. Jacques
after 1773—1804 / *impressed*

547

BOURG LA REINE
J. Jullien & S. Jacques
after 1773—1804 / *impressed*

548

SWINTON
Rockingham Factory
19th cent. / *printed*

549

BOURNEMOUTH
Branksome Ceramics
after 1945 / *printed*

550

BRISTOL
R. Champion
1773—1781 / *red*

551

BRISTOL
Putney & Co.
after 1852 / *printed*

552

BRUSSELS, ETTERBEEK
L. Demeuldre-Coché
1920—1930 / *printed*

553

BRUSSELS, ETTERBEEK
L. Demeuldre-Coché
1920—1941 / *printed*

554

BRUSSELS, ETTERBEEK
L. Demeuldre-Coché
1920—1941 / *printed*

555

BRUSSELS, ETTERBEEK
Etablissements Demeuldre
20th cent. / *printed*

556

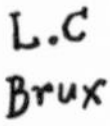

BRUSSELS
L. Cretté
1791—1803 / *red*

557

BUDAPEST
E. Fischer
after 1868 / *printed*

558

SHELTON
Brow, Westerheat & Co.
after 1858 / *printed*

---

559 C

CAUGHLEY
T. Turner
after 1772—1783 / *blue*

---

560 *C*

CHODAU (Chodov)
Hüttner & Co.
1835—1840 / *blue, gold*

---

561 *C*

CHODAU (Chodov)
Haas & Czjizek
after 1905 / *blue*

562

CHODZIEŻ
Fabryka porcelany
after 1882 / *blue*

563

ĆMIELÓW
X. Drucko-Lubecki
after 1842 / *blue*

564

UHLSTÄDT
R. Albert
after 1873 / *blue*

565

LIMOGES
C. Ahrenfeld
after 1894 / *printed*

566

LIMOGES
C. Ahrenfeld
end of 19th cent. / *printed*

---

567 CAEN

CAEN
d'Aigmont-Desmares
1793—1806 / *red*

---

568 **caen**

CAEN
d'Aigmont-Desmares
1793—1806 / *red*

569 

FISCHERN (Rybáře)
C. Knoll
1848—1868 / *impressed*

570 

DELFT
J. Caluve
before 1730 / *impressed*

571 

SHELTON
Cauldon China
20th cent. / *printed*

572 

COALPORT
(COALBROOKDALE)
after 1780 / *blue*

573 

COALPORT
(COALBROOKDALE)
after 1780 / *blue*

574 

COALPORT
(COALBROOKDALE)
after 1780 / *blue*

575 

COALPORT
(COALBROOKDALE)
after 1780 / *blue, gold*

576 

COALPORT
(COALBROOKDALE)
after 1780 / *blue, gold*

577 

NIDERVILLER
A. P. de Custine
1770—1793 / *black*

578 

LUDWIGSBURG
Carl Eugen of Württemberg
1759—1793 / *blue*

579		LUDWIGSBURG Carl Eugen of Württemberg 1759—1793 / *blue*
580		NIDERVILLER A. P. de Custine 1770—1793 / *blue*
581		NIDERVILLER A. P. de Custine 1770—1793 / *blue*
582		LUDWIGSBURG Carl Eugen of Württemberg 1759—1793 / *blue*
583		LUDWIGSBURG Carl Eugen of Württemberg 1759—1806 / *blue*
584		LUDWIGSBURG Carl Eugen of Württemberg 1759—1806 / *blue*
585		ROME F. Cuccumos 1761—1781 / *blue*
586		SCHORNDORF C. M. Bauer & Pfeiffer after 1904—1939 / *printed*
587		COALPORT (COALBROOKDALE) after 1780 / *blue*
588		LIMOGES Grellet Frères after 1771—1796 / *blue, impressed, red, gold*

589	CD	LIMOGES Grellet Frères after 1771—1796 / *blue, impressed, red, gold*
590	C'D	LIMOGES Grellet Frères after 1771—1796 / *blue, impressed, red, gold*
591	C·D	LIMOGES Grellet Frères 1771—1796 / *blue*
592		SORAU (Żary) C. & E. Carstens after 1918 / *printed*
593	C · G W	WÜRZBURG C. Geyger 1775—1780 / *impressed*
594	CF	ZWICKAU C. Fischer after 1850 / *blue*
595	CF	PIRKENHAMMER (Březová) C. Fischer 1846—1857 / *impressed*
596	* CF.....	MILAN San Cristoforo 1830—1833 / *blue*
597	C Flight	WORCESTER J. & J. Flight 1783—1791 / *red, blue*
598	CH	PARIS, BARRIÈRE DE REUILLY H. F. Chanou 1779—1785 / *red, gold*
599	CHAMBERLAINS WORCESTER.	WORCESTER R. Chamberlain after 1840 / *blue*
600	*Chamberlain's Worcester & 63, Piccadilly, London*	WORCESTER Chamberlains after 1840 / *printed*

601

WORCESTER
R. Chamberlain
c. 1850 / *blue*

602

WORCESTER
Chamberlains
1852—1862 / *printed*

603

CHAMBERLAIN & CO.
WORCESTER
155 NEW BOND STREET
& NO. 1
COVENTRY ST
LONDON

WORCESTER
Chamberlains
1840—1845 / *printed*

604

WORCESTER
Chamberlains
1840—1845 / *printed*

605

WORCESTER
Chamberlains
1840—1845 / *printed*

606

CHAMBERLAINS

WORCESTER
Chamberlains
from 1840 / *printed*

607

STOKE-ON-TRENT
Mintons Ltd
from 1911 / *printed*

608

CHANTILLY
Prince de Condé
1760—1800 / *blue*

609
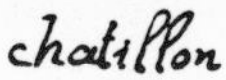

CHATILLON
Porcelain factory
after 1775 / *blue*

610

CHATILLON
Porcelain factory
after 1775 / *blue*

611

CHELSEA
N. Sprimont & C. Gouyn
1745—1749 / *incised*

612

CHODAU (Chodov)
Haas & Czjizek
after 1920 / *impressed*

613

CHODAU (Chodov)
Haas & Czjizek
after 1920 / *printed*

614

CHODAU (Chodov)
Haas & Czjizek
after 1920 / *printed*

615

CHODZIEŻ
Fabryka porcelany
after 1882 / *printed*

616

CHODZIEŻ
Fabryka porcelany
after 1882 / *printed*

617

MANTUA,
CANETTO SULL'OGLIO
Ceramica Furga
after 1872 / *blue*

618

NIDERVILLER
C. Lanfrey
1792—1827 / *blue*

619

NIDERVILLER
C. Lanfrey
1792—1827 / *blue*

620

HOHENBERG
C. M. Hutschenreuther
1865 / *printed*

621

ĆMIELÓW
Fabryka porcelany
1842—1863 / *blue*

622

NIDERVILLER
A. P. de Custine
1770—1802 / *blue*

623

NIDERVILLER
A. P. de Custine
1770—1802 / *blue*

624

COALPORT
Coalport China
2nd half of 19th cent. / *blue*

625

COALPORT
Coalport China
1st half of 20th cent. / *printed*

626

COALPORT
Coalport China
20th cent. / *printed*

627

COALPORT
Coalport China
20th cent. / *printed*

628

HANLEY
Booths & Colclough Ltd.
20th cent. / *printed*

629

HANLEY
Booths & Colclough Ltd.
20th cent. / *printed*

630

HANLEY
Booths & Colclough Ltd.
20th cent. / *printed*

631

LONGTON
Collingwood Bros Ltd.
20th cent. / *printed*

632

STOKE-ON-TRENT
W. T. Copeland
after 1829—20th cent. / *blue*

633

STOKE-ON-TRENT
W. T. Copeland
after 1829—20th cent. / *blue*

634

Copeland late
Spode

STOKE-ON-TRENT
W. T. Copeland
1847—1867 / *blue*

635

STOKE-ON-TRENT
W. T. Copeland
after 1870 / *blue*

636

SPODE
COPELANDS CHINA
ENGLAND

STOKE-ON-TRENT
W. T. Copeland
1847—1867 / *blue*

637

Copeland
Stone China

STOKE-ON-TRENT
W. T. Copeland
1847—1867 / *blue*

638

STOKE-ON-TRENT
W. T. Copeland
20th cent. / *printed*

639

STOKE-ON-TRENT
W. T. Copeland
20th cent. / *printed*

640

STOKE-ON-TRENT
W. T. Copeland & Garrett
1833—1846 / *printed*

641

STOKE-ON-TRENT
W. T. Copeland & Garrett
1833—1846 / *printed*

642

STOKE-ON-TRENT
W. T. Copeland & Garrett
1833—1846 / *printed*

643

STOKE-ON-TRENT
W. T. Copeland & Garrett
1833—1846 / *printed*

644

STOKE-ON-TRENT
W. T. Copeland & Garrett
1833—1846 / *printed*

645

STOKE-ON-TRENT
W. T. Copeland & Garrett
1833—1846 / *printed*

646

STOKE-ON-TRENT
W. T. Copeland & Garrett
1833—1846 / *printed*

647 

STOKE-ON-TRENT
W. T. Copeland & Garrett
1833—1846 / *printed*

---

648 COPELAND & GARRETT

STOKE-ON-TRENT
W. T. Copeland & Garrett
1833—1846 / *printed*

---

649 

COBURG
A. Riemann
after 1860/*printed*

---

650 

CREIDLITZ
Porzellanfabrik A. G.
after 1907 / *printed*

---

651 crepy

CRÉPY EN VALOIS
L. F. Gaignepain & P. Bourgeois
1762—1767 / *incised*

---

652 D, C, P,

CRÉPY EN VALOIS
L. F. Gaignepain & P. Bourgeois
1762—1767 / *incised*

---

653 c. p.

CRÉPY EN VALOIS
L. F. Gaignepain & P. Bourgeois
1762—1767 / *incised*

654
655 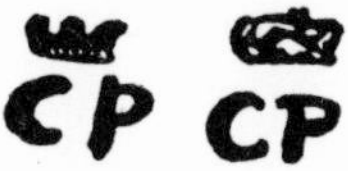

PARIS,
RUE FAUBOURG SAINT DENIS
Comte d'Artois
1779—1793 / *blue, red*

---

656 

ĆMIELÓW
Fabryka porcelany
c. 1850 / *blue*

---

657 

COPENHAGEN
Royal Porcelain Factory
1889 / *green*

658

COPENHAGEN
Dahl-Jensens Porcelaensfabrik
after 1925 / *green*

659

COPENHAGEN
Royal Porcelain Factory
1897 / *green*

660

COPENHAGEN
Royal Porcelain Factory
1923 / *green*

661

COPENHAGEN
Bing & Grøndahl
after 1854 / *blue*

662

COPENHAGEN
Bing & Grøndahl
1905 / *red, various colours*

663

COPENHAGEN
Bing & Grøndahl
1914 / *red, various colours*

664

SCHWARZA-SAALBAHN
E. & A. Müller
after 1890 / *blue*

665

BRUSSELS
L. Cretté
1791—1803 / *blue*

666

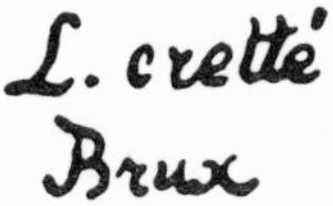

BRUSSELS
L. Cretté
1791—1803 / *red, brown*

667

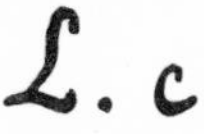

BRUSSELS
L. Cretté
1791—1803 / *red, brown*

668

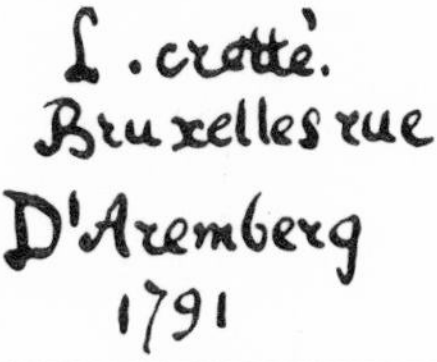

BRUSSELS
L. Cretté
1791—1803 / *red, brown*

669

COALPORT
Caughley, Swansea, Nantgarw
after 1861 / *blue*

670

WALDENBURG (Walbrzych)
C. Tielsch
after 1945 / *blue*

671

POTSCHAPPEL
C. Thieme
after 1872 / *blue*

672

WALDENBURG (Walbrzych)
C. Tielsch
after 1845 / *blue*

673

POTSCHAPPEL
C. Thieme
20th cent. / *printed*

674 

WALDENBURG (Walbrzych)
C. Tielsch
after 1845 / *blue*

675 

KLOSTER VEILSDORF
W. E. von Hildburghausen
before 1765 / *blue*

676 

KLOSTER VEILSDORF
W. E. von Hildburghausen
1760—1797 / *blue*

677 

KLOSTER VEILSDORF
W. E. von Hildburghausen
1760—1797 / *blue*

678 

SCHLACKENWERTH (Ostrov)
Pfeiffer & Löwenstein
after 1918 / *printed*

679 

LUNÉVILLE
P. L. Cyfflé
1766—1780 / *blue*

680 

ALT-ROHLAU (Stará Role)
M. Zdekauer
after 1918 / *printed*

681
682 

DERBY
W. Duesbury & J. Heath
1770—1784 / *gold*

683 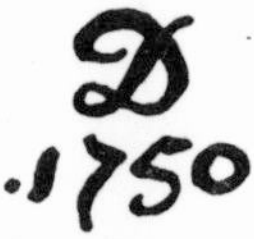

DERBY
W. Duesbury & J. Heath
after 1750 / *incised*

684 

DERBY
W. Duesbury & J. Heath
1770—1784 / *red, gold*

685 

DERBY
W. Duesbury & J. Heath
1770—1784 / *gold*

686

DERBY
W. Duesbury & J. Heath
1784—1811 / *blue, red, gold*

687

DERBY
W. Duesbury
1784—1810 / *incised*

688

DERBY
W. Duesbury
1784—1810 / *blue, red*

689

DERBY
R. Bloor
1811—1848 / *blue, red*

690

DERBY
W. Duesbury
1784—1810 / *blue, red*

691

DERBY
R. Bloor
1811—1848 / *printed, red*

692

DERBY
Stevenson & Handcock
1850—1870 / *red*

693

DRESDEN
19th cent. / *blue*

694

DALLWITZ (Dalovice)
V. W. Lorenz
1831—1850/*impressed*

695

DUISDORF
"Rhenania"
after 1904 / *printed*

696

BRUSSELS, ETTERBEEK
H. Demeuldre
20th cent. / *printed*

697

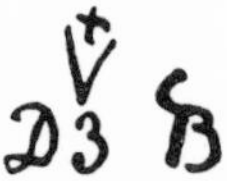

VINOVO
G. Balbo
c. 1800 / *red, green*

698

DALLWITZ (Dalovice)
V. W. Lorenz
1832—1850 / *impressed*

699

STOKE-ON-TRENT
Minton & Boyle
1836—1841 / *printed*

700

COALPORT
(COALBROOKDALE)
end of 18th cent. / *blue*

701

DALLWITZ (Dalovice)
V. W. Lorenz
1832—1850 / *impressed*

702

DALLWITZ (Dalovice)
V. W. Lorenz
1832—1850 / *impressed*

703

DAMM
Steingut- und Porzellanfabrik
1827—1884 / *impressed*

704

COPENHAGEN
Royal Porcelain Factory
1894 / *green, blue*

705

PARIS, RUE DE CHARONNE
Darte Frères
c. 1800 / *red*

706

PARIS, RUE DE CHARONNE
Darte Frères
c. 1800 / *red*

707

LONGPORT
Davenport
1793—1882 / *blue, printed*

708

LONGPORT
Davenport
1793—1882 / *blue, printed*

709

WORCESTER
Flight & Barr
1792—1807 / *incised*

710

COALPORT
(COALBROOKDALE)
c. 1850 / *blue*

711
712

PARIS, CLIGNANCOURT
P. Deruelle
1775—1793 / *red*

713

CRÉPY EN VALOIS
L. Gaignepain & L. Bourgeois
1762—1767 / *blue*

714
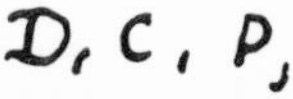

CRÉPY EN VALOIS
L. Gaignepain & L. Bourgeois
1762—1767 / *blue*

715 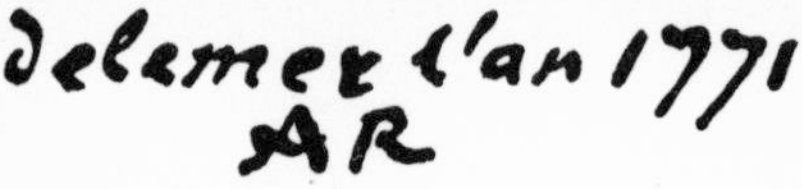

ARRAS
Delemer
1772—1790 / *blue*

716 

COPENHAGEN
Royal Porcelain Factory
1890 / *red, green*

717 

LONGTON
Denton China Company
20th cent. / *printed*

718 

DERBY
A. Planché
1750 / *incised*

719 

DERBY
W. Duesbury
after 1770—1784 / *red*

720 

DERBY
R. Bloor
1850—1870 / *red*

721 

DERBY
R. Bloor
1811—1849 / *blue, red*

722 

DERBY
R. Bloor
1811—1849 / *red*

723 

DERBY
Locker & Co.
1849—1870 / *red*

724

DERBY
Stevenson, Sharp & Co.
1859 / *red*

725

DERBY
W. Duesbury
1784—1810 / *red*

726

DERBY
W. Duesbury
1784—1810 / *red*

727

VINOVO
Dr. V. A. Gioanetti
after 1780 / *blue*

728

CHODAU (Chodov)
J. Hüttner & Co.
1835—1840 / *impressed*

729

MARKTREDWITZ
Jaeger & Co.
after 1872 / *printed*

730

LONGTON
A. T. Finney & Sons Ltd
20th cent. / *printed*

731

PARIS, RUE DE BONDY
J. Dihl
1817—1829 / *blue, red*

732		DERBY W. Duesbury & M. Kean 1795—1796 / *blue, red*
733		DERBY W. Duesbury & M. Kean 1795—1796 / *red, blue*
734 735 736		GRÄFENRODA Dornheim, Koch & Fischer after 1860 / *blue*
737	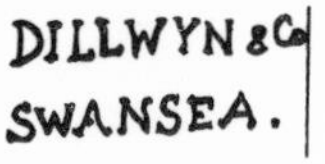	SWANSEA L. W. Dillwyn 1814—1850 / *printed*
738		TIEFENFURTH (Parowa) P. Donath after 1883 / *printed*
739		DUBLIN Donovan & Son beginning of 19th cent. / *red*
740	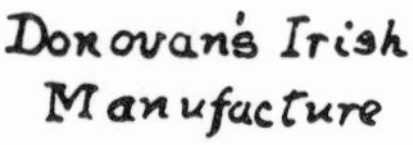	DUBLIN Donovan & Son beginning of 19th cent. / *red, violet*
741		DUBLIN Donovan & Son beginning of 19th cent. / *red*
742		DUBLIN Donovan & Son beginning of 19th cent. / *blue*
743		BURSLEM Doulton & Co. after 1815 / *printed*

744

BURSLEM
Doulton & Co.
after 1815 / *printed*

745

BURSLEM
Doulton & Co.
after 1815 / *printed*

746

BURSLEM
Doulton & Co.
after 1815 / *printed*

747

DRESDEN
19th cent. / *blue*

748

KRONACH
P. Rosenthal & Co.
end of 19th cent. / *blue*

749

LONGTON
Dresden Floral Porcelain Co.
from 1845 / *printed*

750

DRESDEN
Dresdner Porzellanmanufaktur
20th cent. / *printed*

751 

POTSCHAPPEL
C. Thieme
after 1872 / *printed*

752 

DRESDEN
Dresdner Porzellanmanufaktur
20th cent. / *printed*

753 

DERBY
W. Duesbury
1803 / *red*

754 

LONGTON
A. T. Finney & Sons Ltd
20th cent. / *printed*

755 

GATESHEAD
Durham China Company
20th cent. / *printed*

756 

DUISDORF
"Rhenania"
after 1904 / *printed*

757 

MENNECY
Duc de Villeroy
1740—1773 / *incised*

758 

MENNECY
Duc de Villeroy
1734—1740 / *blue and other colours*

759

MENNECY
Duc de Villeroy
1734—1740 / *blue, red, black, brown*

760

MENNECY
Duc de Villeroy
1734—1740 / *red, blue, black, brown*

761

EICHWALD (Dubí)
Bloch & Co.
after 1871 / *blue*

762

EICHWALD (Dubí)
Bloch & Co.
after 1920 / *blue*

763

EICHWALD (Dubí)
Bloch & Co.
c. 1900 / *blue*

764

EISENBERG
F. A. Reinecke
after 1796 / *blue*

765
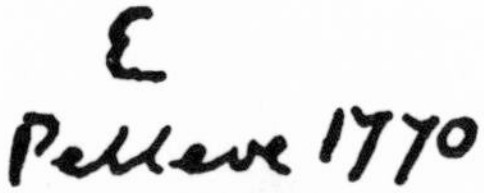

ETIOLLES
D. Pellevé
c. 1770 / *incised*

766
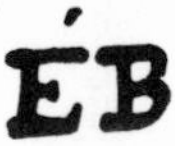

PARIS, RUE DE CRUSSOL
E. Blancheron
1792—1807 / *blue*

767

EISENBERG
Bremer & Schmidt
after 1895 / *printed*

768

DUX (Duchcov)
E. Eichler
after 1860 / *printed*

769

DUX (Duchcov)
E. Eichler
c. 1900 / *printed*

770

POSCHETZAU (Božičany)
Maier & Co.
after 1890 / *printed*

771

EICHWALD (Dubí)
Bloch & Co.
after 1918 / *printed*

772

EICHWALD (Dubí)
Bloch & Co.
after 1871 / *printed*

773

EISENBERG
W. Jäger
after 1867 / *printed*

774

ELGERSBURG
E. & F. C. Arnoldi
after 1808 / *printed*

775

MERKELSGRÜN (Merklín)
"Elsa" Porzellan
1900 until 1918 / *printed*

776

MIDDLETON
c. 1870 / *printed*

777 LONGTON
Cartwright & Edwards Ltd
after 1858 / *printed*

778
779 VOLKSTEDT-RUDOLSTADT
K. Ens
after 1898 / *printed*

780 AICH (Doubí)
"Epiag"
after 1918 / *printed*

781 ALT-ROHLAU (Stará Role)
"Epiag"
after 1918 / *printed*

782 TILLOWITZ (Tulowice)
Reinholdt & Schlegelmilch
after 1869 / *printed*

783 ERBENDORF
C. Seltmann
after 1940 / *printed*

784 ERBENDORF
C. Seltmann
after 1940 / *printed*

785
786 WINDISCH-ESCHENBACH
O. Schaller & Co. and successors
after 1913 / *printed*

787 STADTLENGSFELD
Porzellanfabrik A. G.
c. 1900 / *printed*

788
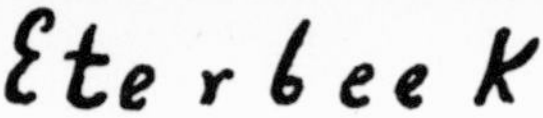
BRUSSELS, ETTERBEEK
C. Kuhne
1787—1803 / *incised*

789
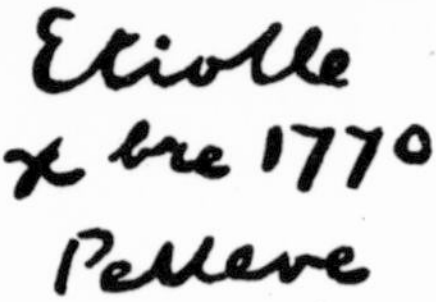
ETIOLLES
D. Pellevé
c. 1770 / *incised*

790
791

FÜRSTENBERG
Charles I of Brunswick
1753—1770 / *blue*

792
793

FÜRSTENBERG
Charles I of Brunswick
1770—1800 / *blue*

794

FÜRSTENBERG
Herzogliche Porzellan-manufaktur
20th cent. / *blue*

795

FÜRSTENBERG
Herzogliche Porzellan-manufaktur
1800—1860 / *blue*

796

WORCESTER
Dr Wall
1751—1783 / *blue*

797

BOW
T. Frye
1755—1760 / *blue*

798

PARIS, RUE DE LA PAIX
J. Feuillet
after 1820 / *green*

799

VOLKSTEDT-RUDOLSTADT
E. Bohne
19th cent. / *blue*

800

FRAUREUTH
Römer & Födisch
2nd half of 19th cent. / *blue*

801 

FRAUREUTH
Römer & Födisch
2nd half of 19th cent. / *blue*

802 

COPENHAGEN
Royal Porcelain Factory
(monogram of Frederick V)
1760—1766 / *blue*

803 

MEISSEN
Frederick Augustus III
after 1733 / *blue*

804 

SELB
P. Müller, "Favorit"
1890—1912 / *printed*

805 

GRÜNSTADT
F. Bartholdi
19th cent. / *blue*

806 

WORCESTER
Flight, Barr & Barr
1813—1840 / *printed, impressed*

807 

WORCESTER
Flight, Barr & Barr
1813—1840 / *impressed*

808 

STADTLENGSFELD
Porzellanfabrik A. G.
after 1889 / *printed*

809 

FULDA
Heinrich VIII von Bibra
1770—1788 / *blue*

810 

FULDA
Adalbert III von Harstall
1788—1789 / *blue*

811
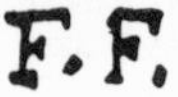

TREVISO
G. & A. Fontebasso
c. 1800 / *blue*

812

SAINT AMAND LES EAUX
J. B. Fauquez
1771—1778 / *blue*

813

DALLWITZ (Dalovice)
F. Fischer
1850—1855 / *impressed*

814

VOLKSTEDT-RUDOLSTADT
F. Greiner
20th cent. / *printed*

815

OBERHOHNDORF
F. Kaestner
1883—20th cent. / *printed*

816

VALENCIENNES
J. B. Fauquez & Lamoninary
1785—1795 / *blue*

817

BUDAU (Budov)
F. Lang
1840—1860 / *impressed*

818

WORCESTER
J. & J. Flight
1783—1792 / *blue*

819
820

WORCESTER
J. & J. Flight
1783—1792 / *red, blue*

821

WORCESTER
J. & J. Flight
1783—1792 / *impressed*

822

WORCESTER
J. & J. Flight
1783—1792 / *blue*

823

WORCESTER
Flight & Barr
1792—1807 / *impressed, printed*

824

WORCESTER
Flight, Barr & Barr
1813—1840 / *impressed, printed*

825

WILHELMSBURG
Aktiengesellschaft
after 1882 / *printed*

826

STOKE-ON-TRENT
Mintons & Hollins
1846—1868 / *printed*

827

PIRKENHAMMER (Březová)
Fischer & Mieg
1810—1846 / *impressed*

828

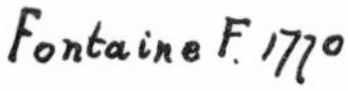

LIMOGES
Grellet Frères & Massié
1770—1796 / *blue*

829

FOËCY
Pillivuyt family
after 1800 / *blue*

830

FOËCY
L. Lourioux
2nd half of 19th cent. / *printed*

831

FENTON
E. Brain & Co.
after 1880 / *printed*

832	ESTABLISHED 18 R & S 50 L FOLEY CHINA	FENTON Robinson & Son after 1850 / *printed*
833		FRAUREUTH Porzellanfabrik after 1866 / *printed*
834	F P Nd. Salzbrunn	NIEDER-SALZBRUNN (Szczawienko) F. Prause from 1899 / *blue*
835 836	F.P.C. F.P.C.	ĆMIELÓW K. Cybulski 1870—1884 / *black, impressed*
837	FPM	FREIWALDAU (Gozdnica) H. Schmidt after 1842 / *blue*
838		NAPLES Ferdinand IV Rex 1772 / *blue*
839	F&R	PIRKENHAMMER (Březová) Fischer & Reichenbach 1811—1845 / *impressed*
840	L L FRANCE	FOËCY L. Lourioux 2nd half of 19th cent. / *printed*
841	F FRAUREUTH	FRAUREUTH Porzellanfabrik after 1866 / *printed*
842	FU	DALLWITZ (Dalovice) F. Urfus 1855—1875 / *impressed*
843	FURGA	MANTUA, CANETTO SULL'OGLIO Ceramica Furga after 1872 / *printed*

844

BOW
E. Heylyn & T. Frye
1748—1755 / *blue*

845
846

VERBILKI
F. Gardner
after 1767—1800 / *blue*

847

GERA
J. G. Ehwaldt, J. Gottbrecht
and successors
1779—1820 / *blue*

848
849

GOTHA
E. Henneberg
1805—1834 / *blue, various colours*

850
851

BERLIN
J. E. Gotzkowsky
1761—1763 / *blue, gold*

852

GEHREN
J. Günthersfeld & Co.
after 1884 / *printed*

853

DOCCIA
Ginori
1884—1888 / *impressed*

854

LE NOVE
G. B. Antonibon
1762—1802 / *blue, impressed*

855

PARIS, RUE DE BONDY
Manufacture du
duc d'Angoulême
1781—1793 / *red, gold, blue*

856

PARIS, RUE DE BONDY
Manufacture du
duc d'Angoulême
1781—1793 / *red, gold*

857

ILMENAU
Galluba & Hofmann
after 1888 / *printed*

858

ILMENAU
Galluba & Hofmann
after 1888 / *printed*

859

GRÜNSTADT
F. Bartholdi
after 1801 / *blue*

860

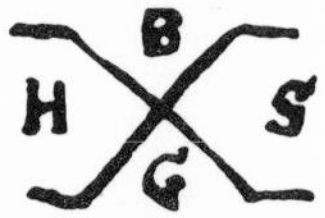

GROSSBREITENBACH
H. Bühl & Söhne
after 1780 / *blue*

861

UPPSALA
"Gefle" Porslin
after 1910 / *printed*

862

UPPSALA
"Gefle" Porslin
after 1910 / *printed*

863

ALT-ROHLAU (Stará Role)
Porzellanfabrik Viktoria A. G.
after 1883 / *printed*

864

GENEVA
J. P. Mühlhauser
1805—1818 / *blue*

865 

GENEVA
J. P. Mühlhauser
1805—1818 / *blue*

866
867 

GERONA
"Cordoba"
19th cent. / *blue, red*

868 

OBERKOTZAU
Greiner & Herda
after 1893 / *printed*

869 

KATOWICE
Giesche
end of 19th cent. / *blue*

870
871 

GIESSHÜBEL (Kysibl)
F. Lehnert
1840—1847 / *impressed*

872 

GIESSHÜBEL (Kysibl)
W. von Neuberg
1846—1902 / *impressed*

873 

DOCCIA
Ginori
1868—1903 / *blue*

874
875 

DOCCIA
Ginori
1868—1903 / *impressed*

876 

DOCCIA
Ginori
1884—1901 / *impressed*

877 

MILAN
Richard —Ginori
1903 / *printed*

878

OESLAU
W. Goebel
after 1879 / *printed*

879

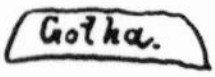

GOTHA
August von Gotha
c. 1805 / *blue*

880

GOTHA
E. Henneberg
middle of 19th cent. / *blue*

881

GOTHA
Morgenroth & Co.
after 1866 / *printed*

882

GOTHA
E. Pfeffer
after 1892 / *blue*

883

UNTERNHAUS
Gerarer Porzellanfabrik
after 1780 /· *blue*

884

GOTHA
E. Pfeffer
after 1892 / *blue*

885

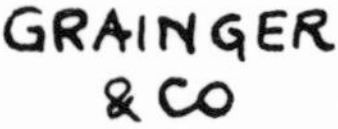

WORCESTER
Grainger & Co.
after 1885 / *blue*

886

WORCESTER
Grainger, Lee & Co.
after 1889 / *blue*

887

GRÄFENTHAL
Weiss, Kühnert & Co.
after 1891 / *printed*

888 

VOLKSTEDT-RUDOLSTADT
W. Greiner
after 1799 / *impressed, blue*

---

889 

GUSTAVSBERG
Ceramic Factory
1845—1880 / *printed*

---

890 

GUSTAVSBERG
Ceramic Factory
1866 / *blue*

---

891 

GUSTAVSBERG
Ceramic Factory
1910—1940 / *blue*

---

892 

GUSTAVSBERG
Ceramic Factory
1930 / *printed*

893
894 

GUSTAVSBERG
Ceramic Factory
1924 / *printed*

---

895 

GUSTAVSBERG
Ceramic Factory
1928 / *printed*

---

896 

GUSTAVSBERG
Ceramic Factory
1930 / *printed*

897
898 

GUSTAVSBERG
Ceramic Factory
1940 / *printed*

899 

GUSTAVSBERG
Ceramic Factory
1943 / *printed*

900 

GEHREN
P. Günthersfeld
after 1884 / *printed*

901
902 

STRASBOURG (HAGENAU)
J. A. Hannong
after 1768—1784 / *blue*

903
904 

STRASBOURG
P. A. Hannong (Hagenau factory)
1783—1784 / *blue*

905 

PARIS, RUE DE FAUBOURG SAINT DENIS
P. A. Hannong
1771—1776 / *blue*

906 

LOWESTOFT
R. Haward
after 1761 / *blue*

907 

MOSCOW
D. Nasonov
1811—1813 / *blue*

908 

LICHTE
Heubach Bros
after 1820 / *blue*

909 

MANNHEIM
Rheinische Porzellanfabrik
19th cent. / *impressed*

910
911 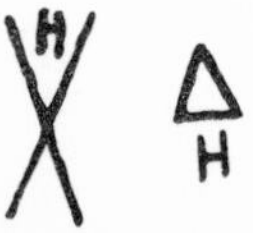

HÜTTENSTEINACH
Schoenau Bros
after 1865 / *blue*

912 

SCHLAGGENWALD (Slavkov)
A. Haas
1847—1867 / *printed*

913 

SCHLAGGENWALD (Slavkov)
A. Haas
1847—1867 / *printed*

914 

SCHLAGGENWALD (Slavkov)
A. Haas
1847—1867 / *printed*

915 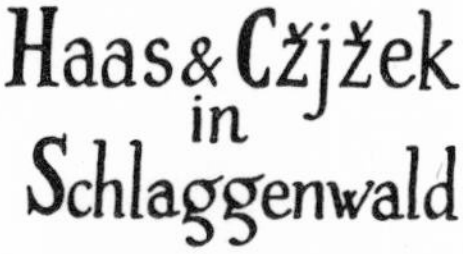

SCHLAGGENWALD (Slavkov)
Haas & Czjizek
after 1867 / *impressed*

916 

HACKEFORS
J. O. Nilson
after 1929 / *printed*

917 

WORCESTER
Hadley
after 1905 / *printed*

918 

ELBOGEN (Loket)
Haidinger Bros
1833—1873 / *impressed*

919 

LONGTON
Hammersley & Co.
1860—1870 / *printed*

920 

LOWESTOFT
R. Haward
after 1761 / *blue*

921 

WALDERSHOF
J. Haviland
1907—1924 / *printed*

922 

KELSTERBACH
Ludwig VIII of Hesse-Darmstadt
1767—1768 / *impressed*

923 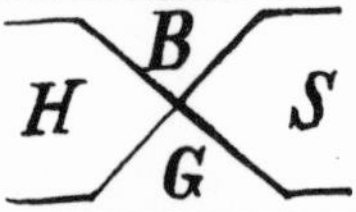

GROSSBREITENBACH
H. Bühl & Söhne
after 1780 / *blue, printed*

924 

KASSEL
Friedrich II of Hesse-Kassel
1766—1788 / *blue*

925 

NEUSTADT
Heber & Co.
after 1900 / *printed*

926 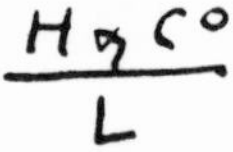

LIMOGES
Haviland & Co.
after 1797 / *blue*

927 

SELB
Heinrich & Co.
after 1896 / *printed*

928 

KELSTERBACH
Ludwig VIII of Hesse-Darmstadt
1767—1768 / *blue*

929 

KELSTERBACH
J. J. Lay
1789—1792 / *incised*

930 

KELSTERBACH
1799—1802 / *blue*

931 

HELSINKI
"Arabia"
after 1948 / *printed*

932

HELSINKI
"Arabia"
after 1948 / *printed*

933

HEREND
Porcelain Factory
1855—1898 / *blue*

934

HEREND
Porcelain Factory
1891—1897 / *blue*

935
936

HEREND
Porcelain Factory
1939 / *blue*

937

HEREND
Porcelain Factory
1940 / *blue*

938

HEREND
Porcelain Factory
1899—1939 / *blue*

939

HEREND
Porcelain Factory
1897—1938 / *blue*

940

HEREND
Porcelain Factory
1941 / *blue*

941

HEREND
Porcelain Factory
1855—1898 / *blue*

942 

HEREND
Porcelain Factory
1933—1938 / *blue*

943 

LICHTE
Heubach Bros
after 1820 / *blue*

944
945 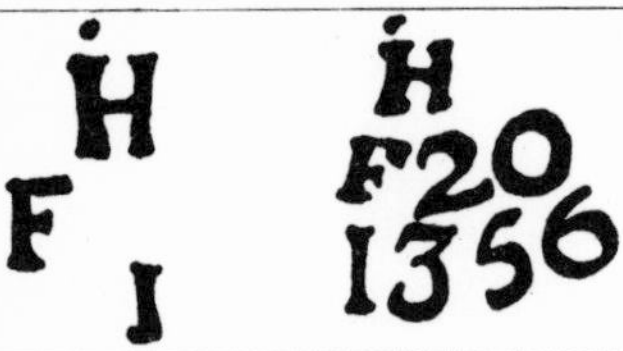

STRASBOURG
J. A. Hannong
1768—1781 / *blue*

946 

FENTON
E. Hughes
after 1883 / *printed*

947 

BOULOGNE
Haffringue
beginning of 19th cent. / *blue*

948 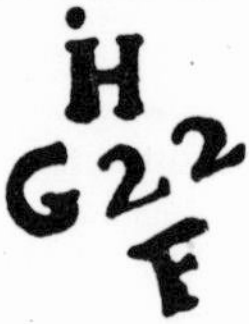

STRASBOURG
J. A. Hannong
1768—1784 / *blue*

949
950 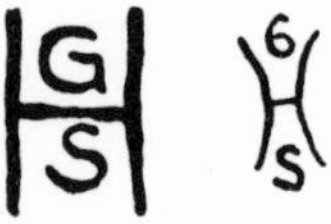

HÜTTENSTEINACH
Schoenau Bros
after 1865 / *blue*

951 

PIRKENHAMMER (Březová)
Friedrich Höcke
1803—1810 / *blue, gold*

952 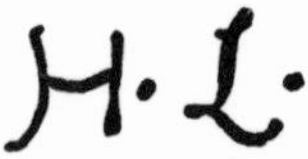

VINCENNES
P. A. Hannong & La Borde
1769—1770 / *blue*

953
954 

VINCENNES
P. A. Hannong & La Borde
1769—1770 / *blue*

955 

LETTIN
H. Baensch
beginning of 20th cent.
printed

956 

COPENHAGEN
J. J. Holm
c. 1780 / *impressed*

957 

LONGTON
Hudson & Middleton
after 1870 / *printed*

958 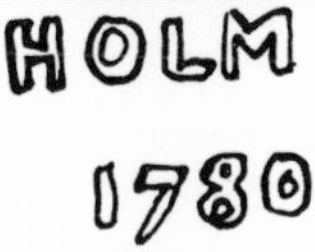

COPENHAGEN
J. J. Holm
c. 1780 / *impressed*

959 

PROBSTZELLA
H. Hutschenreuther
after 1886 / *printed*

960 

VIERZON
Hachez & Pépin
c. 1879 / *blue*

961 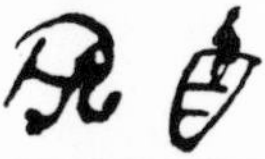

HOHENBERG
C. M. Hutschenreuther
1828—1845 / *impressed*

962 

HOHENBERG
C. M. Hutschenreuther and successors
1890 / *printed*

963 

HOHENBERG
Hutschenreuther
1914 / *printed*

964 

HOHENBERG
Hutschenreuther
1914 / *printed*

965 

HOHENBERG
Hutschenreuther
1914 / *printed*

966
967 

LUBENZ (Žlutice)
H. Reinl
after 1846 / *printed*

968 

UNTERWEISSBACH
H. Schaubach
after 1880 / *printed*

969 

LANE END
Hilditsch & Son
after 1830 / *blue*

970 

SELB
L. Hutschenreuther
after 1856—1920 / *printed*

971 

HÜTTENSTEINACH
Schoenau Bros
after 1865 / *blue*

972 

BOW
W. Duesbury
1760—1776 / *blue*

973 

ILMENAU
C. Nonne
c. 1800 / *blue*

974 

ILMENAU
C. Nonne
1792—1808 / *blue*

975 

SHELTON
J. & W. Ridgeway
until 1830 / *blue*

976 

ILMENAU
Ilmenauer Porzellanfabrik A. G.
1871—1945 / *printed*

977 

ILMENAU
Ilmenauer Porzellanfabrik A. G.
1877—1945 / *blue*

978 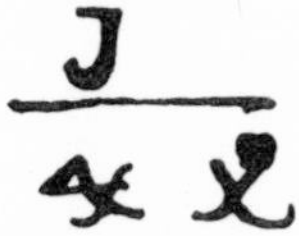

ILMENAU
Ilmenauer Porzellanfabrik A. G.
c. 1790 / *blue*

979 

ILMENAU
Ilmenauer Porzellanfabrik A. G.
before 1785 / *blue*

980 

FRANKENTHAL
J. A. Hannong
1759—1762 / *blue*

981 

BAYREUTH
mark of painter J. A. Fichthorn
1742—1752 / *blue*

982
983

EISENBERG
W. Jäger
after 1867 / *blue*

984
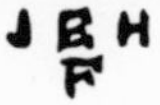

FRIEDLAND (Frýdlant)
J. E. Heintschel
after 1869 / *blue*

985

VIENNA
J. Goldschneider
after 1882 / *blue*

986

987

FRANKENTHAL
J. A. Hannong
1759—1762 / *blue*

988

STRASBOURG
P. A. Hannong
1783—1784 / *impressed*

989

KÖPPELSDORF
J. Hering & Sohn
after 1893 / *printed*

990

ILMENAU
Ilmenauer Porzellanfabrik A. G.
1871—1945 / *printed*

991

ILMENAU
Ilmenauer Porzellanfabrik A. G.
1871—1945 / *printed*

992

VILLEDIEU SUR INDRE
J. Lang
after 1882 / *printed*

993

PARIS, CLIGNANCOURT
J. Moitte
1789—1798 / *blue*

994 

FONTAINEBLEAU
Jacob Petit
after 1834 / *blue*

995 

SCHÖNWALD
J. N. Müller
after 1879 / *blue*

996 

ILMENAU
Ilmenauer Porzellanfabrik A. G.
1871—1945 / *printed*

997 

LIMOGES
J. Pouyat
after 1842 / *blue*

998 

999 

ILMENAU
Ilmenauer Porzellanfabrik A. G.
1871—1945 / *printed*

1000 

1001 

KLAUSENBURG (Cluj)
"Iris" Porcelain
after 1922 / *printed*

1002 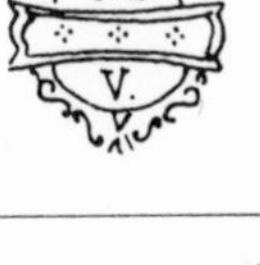

VOHENSTRAUSS
J. Seltmann
after 1910 / *printed*

1003 

1004 

CHARLOTTENBRUNN
(Zofiówka)
J. Schachtel
after 1859 / *printed*

1005

MILAN
G. Richard & Co.
1870—1873 / *printed*

1006

KLÖSTERLE (Klášterec)
M. Weber
1794—1798 / *blue, red*

1007

KLÖSTERLE (Klášterec)
Gräfliche Thun'sche Porzellan-fabrik
1804—1830 / *blue, gold*

1008

KLÖSTERLE (Klášterec)
M. Weber
1794—1798 / *blue*

1009

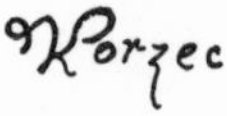

KORZEC
M. Mezer
after 1803 / *red*

1010

KORZEC
M. Mezer
after 1803 / *blue, impressed*

1011

LAUF
F. Krug
after 1871 / *printed*

1012

ELBOGEN (Loket)
H. Kretschmann
c. 1900 / *printed*

1013

OBERHOHNDORF
F. Kaestner
after 1883 / *printed*

1014

KAHLA
Porzellanfabrik
after 1844 / *printed*

1015

EISENBERG
Porzellanfabrik Kalk G. m. b. H.
after 1900 / *printed*

1016

FISCHERN (Rybáře)
C. Knoll
mid-19th cent. / *printed*

1017

FISCHERN (Rybáře)
Karlsbader Porzellanfabrik
beginning of 20th cent.
printed

1018

FISCHERN (Rybáře)
Karlsbader Porzellanfabrik
1900—1910 / *printed*

1019

FISCHERN (Rybáře)
Karlsbader Porzellanfabrik
1st half of 20th cent. / *printed*

1020

FISCHERN (Rybáře)
Karlsbader Porzellanfabrik
1939—1945 / *printed*

1021

FISCHERN (Rybáře)
Karlsbader Porzellanfabrik
c. 1910 / *printed*

1022

FISCHERN (Rybáře)
Karlsbader Porzellanfabrik
beginning of 20th cent.
printed

1023

KARLSKRONA
Karlskrona Porslinsfabrik
after 1918 / *printed*

1024

UPPSALA
Karlskrona Porslinsfabrik
after 1945 / *printed*

1025

KATZHÜTTE
J. W. Hamann
19th cent. / *printed*

1026

KATZHÜTTE
Hertwig & Co.
after 1945 / *printed*

1027

WORCESTER
Kerr & Binns
1852—1862 / *printed*

1028

OHRDRUF
Kestner
20th cent / *printed*

1029

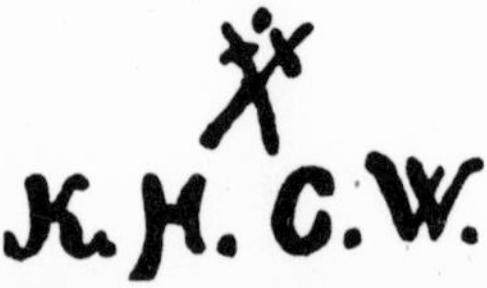

MEISSEN
Königliche Hofconditorei
Warschau
1713—1806 / *various colours*

1030

LANGEWIESEN
O. Schlegelmilch
after 1842 / *printed*

1031

COPENHAGEN
Bing & Grøndahl
after 1905 / *printed*

1032

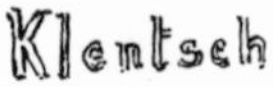

KLENTSCH (Kleneč)
A. Schmidt
1835—1889 / *impressed*

1033

WISTRITZ (Bystřice)
Krantzberger, Mayer & Purkert
after 1911 / *printed*

1034

KÖNIGSZELT (Jaworzyna Śląska)
Porcelain Factory
after 1860 / *printed*

1035

KÖNIGSZELT (Jaworzyna Śląska)
Porcelain Factory
after 1860 / *printed*

1036

CHODAU (Chodov)
J. Hüttner & Co.
1835—1840 / *impressed*

1037

KÖPPELSDORF
J. Hering & Sohn
after 1893 / *printed*

1038

KORZEC
Mérault & Petion
1822 / *red*

1039

KORZEC
Mérault & Petion
1830 / *red*

1040

KORZEC
M. Mezer
beginning of 19th cent. / *red*

1041
1042

KORZEC
M. Mezer
beginning of 19th cent. / *red*

1043

KORZEC
F. Mezer
1793—1814 / *blue*

1044

KORZEC
F. Mezer
1st half of 19th cent. / *gold*

1045

EISENBERG
Porzellanfabrik Kalk G. m. b. H.
after 1900 / *printed*

1046

MEISSEN
Königl. Porzellanmanufaktur
from 1722 / *blue*

1047

MEISSEN
Königl. Porzellanmanufaktur
1723—1724 / *blue*

1048

MEISSEN
Königl. Porzellanmanufaktur
1723—1724 / *blue*

1049

MEISSEN
Königl. Porzellanmanufaktur
1723—1724 / *blue*

1050 

BERLIN
Königl. Porzellanmanufaktur
1823—1832 / *blue*

1051 

WALDENBURG (Walbrzych)
Krister Porzellanmanufaktur
1831—1945 / *printed*

1052 

WALDENBURG (Walbrzych)
Krister Porzellanmanufaktur
until 1945 / *printed*

1053 

BERLIN
Königl. Porzellanmanufaktur
1844—1847 / *blue*

1054 

BERLIN
Königl. Porzellanmanufaktur
from 1857 / *blue*

1055 

SCHEIBE-ALSBACH
A. W. F. Kister
after 1837 / *blue*

1056 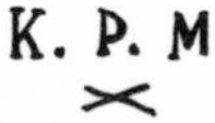

SCHEIBE-ALSBACH
A. W. F. Kister
after 1831 / *blue*

1057 

WALDENBURG (Walbrzych)
Krister Porzellanmanufaktur
after 1900 / *blue*

1058
1059

WALDENBURG (Walbrzych)
Krister Porzellanmanufaktur
after 1831 / *blue*

1060 

BERLIN
Königl. Porzellanmanufaktur
1837—1844 / *blue*

1061 

WALDENBURG (Walbrzych)
Krister Porzellanmanufaktur
19th cent. / *blue*

1062 

SELB
Krautheim & Adelberg
after 1884 / *printed*

1063 

SELB
Krautheim & Adelberg
after 1884 / *printed*

1064 

WISTRITZ (Bystřice)
Krantzberger, Mayer & Purkert
after 1911 / *printed*

1065 

LANDSTUHL
Krister Porzellanmanufaktur
after 1952 / *printed*

1066 

KRONACH
Stockhardt & Schmidt-Eckert
after 1912 / *printed*

1067
1068 

BLANKENHAIN
E. Krüger
after 1847 / *printed*

1069 

TIEFENFURTH (Parowa)
K. Steinmann G. m. b. H.
1883—1932 / *printed*

1070 

WALDENBURG (Walbrzych)
Krister Porzellanmanufaktur
19th cent. / *blue*

1071 

LUDWIGSBURG
Ludwig Eugen of Württemberg.
1793—1795 / *blue*

1072
1073
1074 

LILLE
Leperre-Durot
1784—1817 / *blue*

1075 

ORLÉANS
Benoist Le Brun
1806—1812 / *red*

1076
1077 

SCHORNDORF
Bauer & Pfeiffer
1904—1939 / *printed*

1078 

PARIS, GROS CAILLOU
J. Jacquemart (L. Broillet)
1765—1773 / *blue*

1079 

VALENCIENNES
J. B. Fauquez & Lamoninary
1785—1795 / *blue*

1080
1081
1082 

PARIS, RUE DE REUILLY
J. J. Lassia
1774—1784 / *red, gold*

1083 

PASSAU
Lenck family
2nd half of 19th cent. / *printed*

1084 

LIMBACH
G. Greiner
1772—1787 / *blue*

1085 

VALENCIENNES
J. B. Fauquez & Lamoninary
1785—1795 / *blue*

1086 1087		LETTIN H. Baensch 1858—1945 / *printed*
1088		LUDWIGSBURG Ludwig Eugen of Württemberg 1793—1795 / *blue*
1089		LANGEWIESEN O. Schlegelmilch after 1892 / *printed*
1090	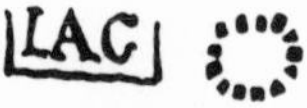	LISBON J. J. Paszoa after 1870 / *printed*
1091		KRUMMENNAAB H. Lange & Co. after 1934 / *printed*
1092 1093		LUXEMBOURG Bloch Sept Fontaines 19th cent. / *blue*
1094 1095		LUXEMBOURG Bloch Sept Fontaines 19th cent. / *blue*
1096		LASSAY Comte de Lauraguais-Brancas 1763—1768 / *blue, various colours*
1097		LUXEMBOURG Bloch Sept Fontaines 19th cent. / *blue, various colours*
1098		LUXEMBOURG Bloch Sept Fontaines 19th cent. / *blue*

1099 

LUXEMBOURG
Bloch Sept Fontaines
19th cent. / *impressed*

1100
1101 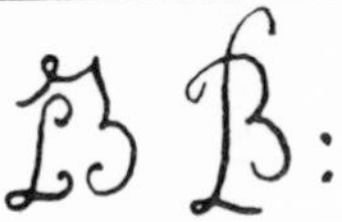

LASSAY
Comte de Lauraguais-Brancas
1763—1768 / *incised*

1102 

LIMBACH
G. Greiner
1762—1787 / *incised*

1103 

LIMBACH
G. Greiner
1762—1787 / *blue*

1104 

ORLÉANS
Benoist Le Brun
1806—1812 / *blue*

1105
1106 

BRUSSELS
L. Cretté
1791—1803 / *blue*

1107 

BRUSSELS
L. Cretté
1791—1803 / *blue*

1108 

BRUSSELS
L. Cretté
1791—1803 / *blue*

1109 

BRUSSELS
L. Cretté
1791—1803 / *blue*

1110 

DERBY
Royal Crown Porcelain Co.
from 1876 / *printed*

1111 

LETTIN
H. Baensch
after 1858 / *blue*

1112 

LETTIN
Porzellanfabrik
after 1945 / *printed*

1113
1114 

LETTIN
H. Baensch
after 1858 / *blue*

1115 

KAHLA
C. A. Lehmann & Sohn
after 1895 / *printed*

1116 

LICHTE
Heubach Bros
after 1820 / *blue*

1117 

SCHLAGGENWALD (Slavkov)
J. Lippert & A. Haas
1830—1846 / *impressed*

1118 

SELB
L. Hutschenreuther
after 1920—1938 / *printed*

1119 

ALT-ROHLAU (Stará Role)
J. Schneider & Co.
after 1904 / *blue*

1120

LILLE
Leperre-Durot
1784—1817 / *blue, red, gold*

1121

LIMBACH
Greiner family
1882 / *printed*

1122
1123

LIMBACH
Greiner family
1882 / *printed*

1124

LIMOGES
Royal Porcelain Factory
J. F. Alluaud
1788—1793 / *blue*

1125

LIMOGES
Royal Porcelain Factory
1784—1796 / *blue, red, gold*

1126

LIMOGES
J. Pouyat
after 1842 / *green*

1127

LIMBACH
G. Greiner
1772—1787 / *blue*

1128

LIMBACH
G. Greiner
1772—1787 / *blue*

1129

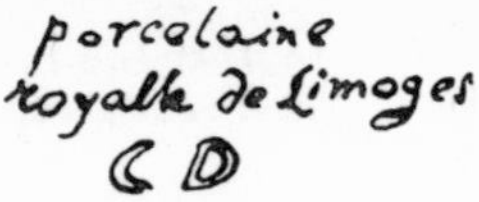

LIMOGES
Royal Porcelain Factory
Comte d'Artois
1771—1784 / *blue, red, gold, incised*

1130

LIMOGES
H. A. Balleroy Frères
19th cent. / *blue*

1131

LIMOGES
J. Balleroy & Co.
19th cent. / *blue*

1132

LIMOGES
L. Bernardaux & Co.
after 1863 / *blue*

1133

LIMOGES
L. Bernardaux & Co.
after 1863 / *printed*

1134

LIMOGES
Beulé, Reboisson & Parot
19th cent. / *blue, printed*

1135

LIMOGES
Fontanille & Marraud
after 1925 / *printed*

1136

LIMOGES
Fontanille & Marraud
19th cent. / *printed*

1137

LIMOGES
Granger & Co.
19th cent. / *printed*

1138
1139

LIMOGES
Guérin-Pouyat-Elite
19th cent. / *printed*

1140

LIMOGES
Guérin-Pouyat-Elite
19th cent. / *printed*

1141

LIMOGES
Haviland & Co.
after 1924 / *printed*

1142

LIMOGES
Haviland & Co.
after 1924 / *printed*

1143
1144

LIMOGES
A. Lanternier & Co.
after 1855 / *printed*

1145
1146

LIMOGES
La Porcelaine Limousine
19th cent. / *printed*

1147
1148

LIMOGES
C. Martin & Duché
19th cent. / *printed*
20th cent. / *printed*

1149

LIMOGES
Merlin-Lemas
19th cent. / *blue*

1150

LIMOGES
Vogt & Dose
before 1919 / *printed*

1151

LIMOGES
Raynaud & Co.
1919 / *printed*

1152

LIMOGES
Raynaud & Co.
after 1919 / *printed*

1153

LIMOGES
Rousset & Guillerot
20th cent. / *printed*

1154

LIMOGES
Societé Porcelainière de Limoges
20th cent. / *printed*

1155

LIMOGES
Fabrique de Porcelaines Blanches & Décorées Anciens Ets.
after 1908 / *printed*

1156

LIMOGES
Touze, Lemaître Frères & Blancher
19th cent. / *printed*

1157
1158

LIMOGES
Union Céramique
19th cent. / *printed*

1159
1160

LIMOGES
Union Limousine
after 1908 / *printed*

1161

LIMOGES
A. Vignaud
after 1911 / *printed*

1162

LIMOGES
Villegoureix
19th cent. / *printed*

1163

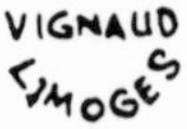

LIMOGES
A. Vignaud
after 1911 / *blue*

1164

LIMOGES
Villegoureix
19th cent. / *printed*

1165

SCHLAGGENWALD (Slavkov)
J. Lippert & A. Haas
1830—1846 / *impressed*

1166

SCHLAGGENWALD (Slavkov)
J. Lippert & A. Haas
1830—1846 / *printed*

1167

LISBON
J. M. Perreira
end of 18th cent. / *gold, red*

1168

LIMOGES
Manuf. de Porcelaines Ets.
Legrand
19th cent. / *printed*

1169

LIMBACH
G. Greiner
1772—1787 / *blue*

1170
1171

VINCENNES
Royal Porcelain Factory
1740—1752 / *blue*

1172

VINCENNES
Royal Porcelain Factory
1740—1752 / *blue*

1173

VINCENNES
Royal Porcelain Factory
1740—1752 / *blue*

1174

VINCENNES
Royal Porcelain Factory
1740—1752 / *gold*

1175

VINCENNES
Royal Porcelain Factory
1753—1756 / *blue*

1176

VINCENNES
Royal Porcelain Factory
1754 / *blue*

1177

VINCENNES
Royal Porcelain Factory
1755 / *blue*

1178

VINCENNES
Royal Porcelain Factory
1740—1752 / *blue*

1179

VINCENNES
Royal Porcelain Factory
1753—1756 / *blue*

1180

SÈVRES
Royal Porcelain Factory
1778 / *blue, various colours*

1181

SÈVRES
Royal Porcelain Factory
(hard-paste)
1756 / *blue, various colours*

1182

SÈVRES
Royal Porcelain Factory
(hard-paste)
1769—1793 / *blue, various colours*

1183

COALPORT
imitation of Sèvres mark
1860—1880 / *blue*

1184

FOËCY
L. Lourioux
19th cent. / *printed*

1185

FENTON
E. Hughes
after 1883 / *printed*

1186

LONGTON
Hammersley & Co.
c. 1900 / *printed*

1187

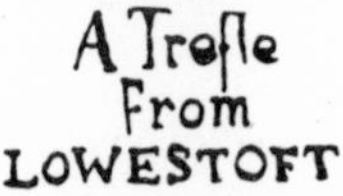

LOWESTOFT
R. Allen
after 1802 / *blue*

1188

LOWESTOFT
James & Mary Curtis
after 1757—1771 / *black*

1189

VINCENNES
Louis Philippe, duc de Chartres
1777—1788 / *blue*

1190

PARIS, RUE AMELOT
under the aegis of Louis Philippe, duc d'Orléans
1786—1793 / *blue*

1191 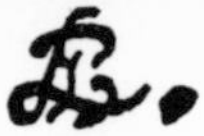

ORLÉANS
Benoist Le Brun
1806—1812 / *red*

1192 

VINCENNES
Louis Philippe, duc de Chartres
1777—1788 / *blue*

1193 

BORDEAUX
Lahens & Rateau
after 1819 / *blue*

1194 

LA SEYNIE
Marquis de Beaupoil & Co.
1774—1789 / *blue, red*

1195 

LA SEYNIE
E. Baignol
1789—1856 / *blue, red*

1196 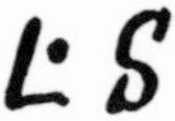

LA SEYNIE
E. Baignol
1789—1856 / *blue, red*

1197 

VENDRENNES
M. Lozelet
after 1800 / *blue*

1198 

LUBARTÓW
Count H. Lubieński
1840—1850 / *impressed*

1199 

LUBARTÓW
Count H. Lubieński
1840—1850 / *impressed*

1200 

LUBARTÓW
Count H. Lubieński
1840—1850 / *impressed*

1201 

PODERSAM (Podbořany)
Porzellanfabrik "Alp" G. m. b. H.
1920—1941 / *printed*

1202 

SCHORNDORF
Bauer & Pfeiffer
1904—1939 / *printed*

1203 

VINOVO
G. Lormello
1815—1820 / *blue*

1204 

VALENCIENNES
Lamoninary
1800—1810 / *blue, red, brown, black*

1205 

VALENCIENNES
Lamoninary
1800—1810 / *blue, red, brown, black*

1206 

SCHORNDORF
Bauer & Pfeiffer
1904—1939 / *printed*

1207 

SCHORNDORF
Bauer & Pfeiffer
1904—1939 / *printed*

1208 

FLORENCE
Francesco II Medici
1578—1587 / *blue*

1209 

VOLKSTEDT-RUDOLSTADT
G. H. Macheleid
1760—1762 / *violet*

1210 

PARIS, CLIGNANCOURT
Fabrique de Monsieur
1775—1793 / *red*

1211
1212

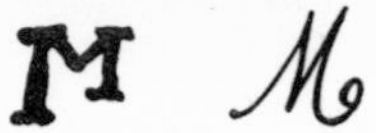

PARIS, CLIGNANCOURT
J. Moitte
1793—1798 / *blue*

1213

SCHWARZA-SAALBAHN
E. & A. Müller
after 1890 / *blue*

1214
1215

STOKE-ON-TRENT
T. Minton
1793—1835 / *various colours, gold*

1216

HANLEY
Booths & Colclough Ltd.
20th cent. / *printed*

1217

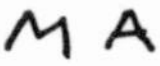

CHANTILLY
M. Aron Père
after 1845 / *printed*

1218

MAYERHÖFEN
Benedikt Bros
1883—1918 / *printed*

1219

MÄBENDORF
Mathes & Ebel
after 1882 / *printed*

1220
1221

MÄBENDORF
Mathes & Ebel
after 1882 / *printed*

1222
1223

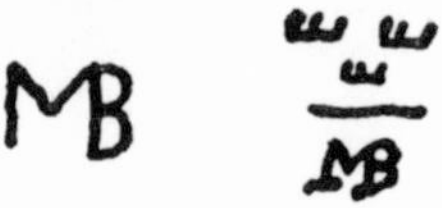

MARIEBERG
P. Berthevin
1766—1769 / *incised*

1224

MARIEBERG
P. Berthevin
1766—1769 / *incised*

1225

MARIEBERG
H. Sten and J. Dortu
1777—1778 / *blue*

1226

ELGERSBURG
E. & F. C. Arnoldi
after 1808 / *blue*

1227

HOHENBERG
C. M. Hutschenreuther
1860 / *impressed*

1228
1229

LA MONCLOA
Royal Porcelain Factory
1817—1850 / *red*

1230

MEHUN-SUR-YÈVRE
Pillivuyt & Co.
after 1853 / *blue*

1231

EICHWALD (Dubí)
Dr Widera & Co.; imitation of Meissen with onion pattern
19th—20th cent. / *blue*

1232

KÖNITZ
Metzel Bros
after 1909 / *blue*

1233

LUBAU (Hlubany)
Martin Bros
after 1874 / *blue*

1234

KÖNITZ
Metzel Bros
1909—1950 / *blue*

1235

KÖNITZ
Metzel Bros
1909—1950 / *blue*

1236

MILAN
S. Richard
after 1883 / *blue*

1237

DELFT
Ary de Milde
end of 17th cent. / *impressed*

1238
1239

STOKE-ON-TRENT
T. Minton and successors
1941 / *printed*

1240

HANLEY
"Blue Mist"
20th cent. / *printed*

1241
1242

MITTERTEICH
Porzellanfabrik
after 1917 / *printed*

1243

MITTERTEICH
Porzellanfabrik
after 1917 / *printed*

1244

SÈVRES
period of the Consulate
1803—1804 / *red, printed*

1245

ILMENAU
Metzler Bros & Ortloff
after 1875 / *blue*

1246

PARIS, RUE AMELOT
Manufacture du duc d'Orléans
(J. B. Outrequin)
1786—1793 / *red, gold*

1247

MOABIT
M. Schuman & Sohn
1835 / *blue*

1248

OUDE LOOSDRECHT
J. de Mol
1771—1784 / *incised*

1249

OUDE LOOSDRECHT
J. de Mol
1771—1784 / *black, various colours*

1250

OUDE LOOSDRECHT
J. de Mol
1771—1784 / *red, various colours*

1251

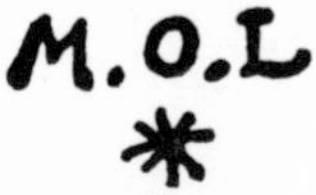

OUDE LOOSDRECHT
Manufacture Oude Loosdrecht
after 1784 / *blue, gold*

1252

OUDE LOOSDRECHT
J. de Mol
1771—1784 / *impressed*

1253

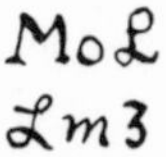

OUDE LOOSDRECHT
J. de Mol
1771—1784 / *violet*

1254

OUDE LOOSDRECHT
J. de Mol
1771—1784 / *blue, impressed*

1255

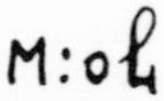

OUDE LOOSDRECHT
J. de Mol
1771—1784 / *impressed*

1256	A M:oL	OUDE LOOSDRECHT J. de Mol 1771—1784 / *blue*
1257	M·OL L27	OUDE LOOSDRECHT J. de Mol 1771—1784 / *gold, violet*
1258	M: o:L 87	OUDE LOOSDRECHT Manufacture Oude Loosdrecht after 1784 / *blue*
1259	MO Moitte	PARIS, CLIGNANCOURT J. Moitte 1793—1798 / *blue*
1260 1261	M O I M&O	ILMENAU Metzler Bros & Ortloff after 1875 / *printed*
1262	MONCLOA	LA MONCLOA Royal Porcelain Factory 1817—1850 / *impressed*
1263	MOSA MAASTRICHT (FABRIEKSMERK)	MAASTRICHT L. Regout & Zonen after 1883 / *printed*
1264	PM Moschendorf BAVARIA	HOF-MOSCHENDORF O. Reinecke after 1878 / *printed*
1265 1266	MP· MP	ETIOLLES J. B. Monier & D. Pellevé 1768—1770 / *incised*
1267	M.P.M.	MEISSEN Meissener Porzellanmanufaktur after 1722 / *blue*

1268

MAASTRICHT
Manufaktur Porselein Mosa
after 1883 / *printed*

1269

BAYREUTH
S. P. Meyer
after 1900 / *printed*

1270

VOLKSTEDT-RUDOLSTADT
Müller & Co.
after 1907 / *printed*

1271

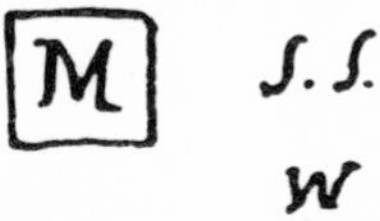

VOLOKITINO
A. Miklaszewski
1820—1864 / *printed*

1272
1273

NAPLES
Royal Porcelain Factory
1771—1834 / *blue, impressed*

1274
1275

NAPLES
Royal Porcelain Factory
1771—1834 / *blue, impressed*

1276

NAPLES
Royal Porcelain Factory
1771—1834 / *blue*

1277

SÈVRES
2nd Empire period
1852—1870 / *red*

1278

DOCCIA
casts of Capodimonte models
1850—1903 / *blue*

1279
1280

LE NOVE
Antonibon family
end of 18th—19th cent.
incised

1281

NIDERVILLER
A. P. de Custine—C. F. Lanfrey
1780—1800 / *black*

1282

SHELTON, NEW HALL
New Hall China Factory
1781—1825 / *blue*

1283
1284

ALT-HALDENSLEBEN
Nathusius
after 1826 / *blue*

1285

VOLKSTEDT-RUDOLSTADT
E. Bohne & Söhne
1854—1900 / *blue*

1286

VOLKSTEDT-RUDOLSTADT
K. Ens
after 1898 / *blue*

1287

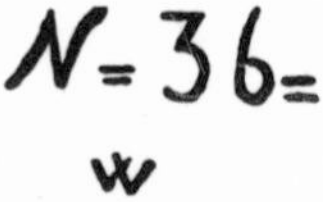

MEISSEN
Königliche Porzellanmanufaktur
numbered white porcelain to
no. 68
before 1725 / *blue*

1288

CHELSEA
19th cent. / *impressed*

1289

NANTGARW
W. Billingsley & S. Walker
1813—1822 / *blue*

1290

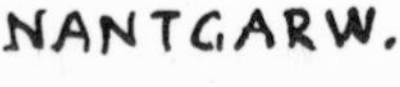

NANTGARW
W. Billingsley & S. Walker
1813—1822 / *impressed*

1291 

PARIS, RUE POPINCOURT
J. N. H. Nast
1782—1835 / *red, gold*

1292 

PARIS, RUE POPINCOURT
J. N. H. Nast
1782—1835 / *red, gold*

1293 

COALPORT
Coalport, Nantgarw, Swansea
1861 / *gold*

1294 

SHELTON, NEW HALL
Hollins & Warburton
c. 1800 / *printed*

1295 

VOLKSTEDT-RUDOLSTADT
K. Ens
after 1898 / *blue*

1296 

LUNÉVILLE
P. L. Cyfflé
1769—1780 / *blue*

1297 

1298 

GIESSHÜBEL (Kysibl)
W. von Neuberg
1847—1902 / *impressed*

1299 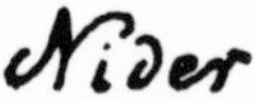

NIDERVILLER
A. P. de Custine—C. F. Lanfrey
1780—1800 / *black*

1300 

NIDERVILLER
A. P. de Custine—C. F. Lanfrey
end of 18th cent. / *impressed*

1301 

NIDERVILLER
A. P. de Custine—C. F. Lanfrey
1780—1800 / *black*

1302

LE NOVE
Antonibon family
from 1781 / *gold*

1303

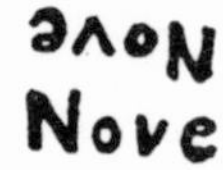

LE NOVE
Antonibon family
1763—1773 / *relief*

1304

LE NOVE
Antonibon family
from 1781 / *incised*

1305

LE NOVE
G. Baroni
1802—1825 / *various colours*

1306

LE NOVE
G. Baroni
1802—1825 / *impressed*

1307

LE NOVE
G. B. Antonibon
from 1762 / *gold, various colours*

1308

LE NOVE
Antonibon family
1762—1802 / *red*

1309

LE NOVE
G. Baroni
1802—1825 / *blue*

1310

LE NOVE
G. Baroni
1802—1825 / *blue*

1311

NOVI SAD
Fabrika porculana
after 1922 / *printed*

1312

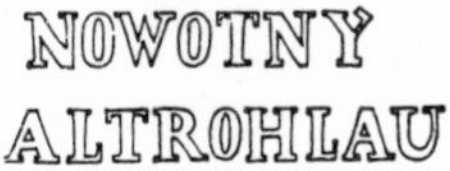

ALT-ROHLAU (Stará Role)
A. Nowotny
1838—1884 / *impressed*

1313

ILMENAU
C. Nonne & K. Roesch
1808—1871 / *printed*

1314

OTTWEILER
Prince of Nassau-Saarbrücken
1763—1794 / *blue, gold*

1315

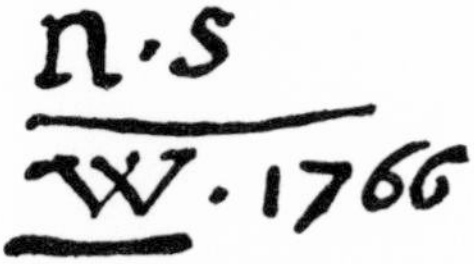

OTTWEILER
Prince of Nassau-Saarbrücken
(manager H. Wagner)
1766 / *incised*

1316

ALT-ROHLAU (Stará Role)
O. & E. Gutherz
1899—1918 / *printed*

1317

OHRDRUF
Baehr & Proeschild
after 1871 / *printed*

1318

OISSEL
La Céramique "Normande"
20th cent. / *printed*

1319 

ORLÉANS
G. d'Aureaubert
1753—1783 / *blue*

1320 

BOURG LA REINE
J. Jullien & S. Jacques
1773—1804 / *printed*

1321 

TRIPTIS
Triptis A. G. Porzellanfabrik
after 1891/*printed*

1322 

TRIPTIS
Triptis A. G. Porzellanfabrik
after 1891 / *printed*

1323 
1324 

PRAGUE
K. Kriegel & Co.
after 1837 / *impressed*

1325 

KORZEC
Merault & Petion
1815—1929 / *blue*

1326 

KORZEC
Petion
1815—1829 / *blue, red, gold, impressed*

1327 

LORIENT
Charey, Sauvageau & Hervé
c. 1800 / *blue*

1328 
1329 

PINXTON
W. Billingsley & J. Coke
1796—1813 / *red*

1330 

ETIOLLES
D. Pellevé
1768—1770 / *incised*

1331 

SCHMIEDEBERG (Kowary)
Pohl Bros
after 1871 / *blue*

1332 

PROBSTZELLA
H. Hutschenreuther
after 1886 / *printed*

1333 

HELSINKI
"Arabia"
after 1948 / *printed*

1334 

ILMENAU
A. Fischer
after 1907 / *printed*

1335 

SCHELTEN (Šelty)
J. Palme
after 1829 / *impressed*

1336 

SCHELTEN (Šelty)
J. Palme
after 1829 / *printed*

1337 

SCHELTEN (Šelty)
J. Palme
1851—1860 / *printed*

1338 

LONGTON
Paragon China Ltd
after 1919 / *printed*

1339 

PARIS, RUE DU PETIT CARROUSEL
C. B. Guy
1789—1800 / *red, gold*

1340 

PARIS, RUE THIROUX
Housel & Guy
1797—1798 / *red*

1341

PARIS, RUE DE BONDY
Manufacture du duc d'Angoulême
1781—1793 / *red*

1342

PARIS, RUE DE BONDY
J. Dihl & Guerhard
1793—1817 / *red*

1343

PARIS, RUE POPINCOURT
J. N. H. Nast
1782—1835 / *incised*

1344

PARIS, RUE DE CRUSSOL
C. Potter & Blancheron
1792—beginning of 19th cent.
blue

1345

IRÚN
Luso Espanola de Porcelanas, Fabrica de Bidosa
after 1935 / *printed*

1346

CREIDLITZ
Porzellanfabrik A. G.
after 1907 / *printed*

1347

PARIS, RUE DU PETIT CARROUSEL
C. B. Guy
1789—1800 / *red, gold*

1348

GOTHA
E. Pfeffer
after 1892 / *printed*

1349

GEHREN
Porzellanfabrik Günthersfeld A. G.
after 1884 / *printed*

1350

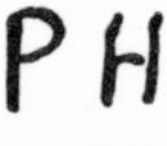

STRASBOURG
Paul A. Hannong
1751—1754 / *incised, blue*

1351	PH	STRASBOURG Paul A. Hannong 1751—1754 / *impressed*
1352		STRASBOURG (HAGENAU) Pierre A. Hannong (Hagenau factory) 1783—1784 / *blue*
1353	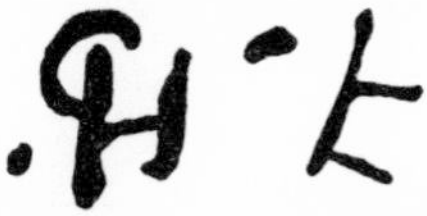	STRASBOURG (HAGENAU) Pierre A. Hannong (Hagenau factory) 1783—1784 / *incised*
1354 1355	PHF PH F	FRANKENTHAL Paul A. Hannong 1755—1759 / *impressed*
1356	PICKMAN Y.CA. CHINA OPACA SEVILLA	SEVILLE "La Cartuja"; de Aponte, Pickmann & Co. after 1867 / *printed*
1357	PICKMANN Y C CHINA OPACA	SEVILLE "La Cartuja"; de Aponte, Pickmann & Co. after 1867 / *printed*
1358	AP&F France C. H. PILLIVUYT & Cie Paris. PARIS. FOESCY. MEHUN.	FOËCY C. H. Pillivuyt 2nd half of 19th cent. / *printed*
1359	PILIVITE PORCELAINES A FEU PILLIVUYT&Cie MEHUN FRANCE	MEHUN-SUR-YÈVRE C. H. Pillivuyt after 1852 / *printed*
1360	PINK Vogue BONE CHINA MADE IN ENGLAND	HANLEY Booths & Colclough Ltd 19th cent. / *printed*

1361

PIRKENHAMMER (Březová)
"Epiag"
1918—1938 / *printed*

1362

KORZEC
Petion
1815—1828 / *red*

1363

PARIS, RUE AMELOT
Manufacture du duc d'Orléans
1786—1793 / *blue*

1364

KRUMMENNAAB
Illinger & Co.
after 1931 / *printed*

1365

KALTENHOF (Oblanov)
J. Dietel
1918—1938 / *printed*

1366

STADTLENGSFELD
Porzellanfabrik A. G.
after 1889 / *printed*

1367

PLANKENHAMMER
Fross Bros
after 1908 / *printed*

1368

LONGTON
R. H. Plant & Co.
after 1880 / *printed*

1369

SCHLACKENWERTH (Ostrov)
Pfeiffer & Löwenstein
20th cent. / *printed*

1370

SCHLACKENWERTH (Ostrov)
Pfeiffer & Löwenstein
20th cent. / *printed*

1371

HOF MOSCHENDORF
O. Reinecke
after 1878 / *printed*

1372

POSCHETZAU (Božičany)
Maier & Co.
1938—1945 / *printed*

1373

OBERKOTZAU
Neuerer K. G.
after 1943 / *printed*

1374

PONTENX
De Rosly
1779—1790 / *blue*

1375

POTSCHAPPEL
C. Thieme
after 1872 / *printed*

1376

POTSCHAPPEL
C. Thieme
after 1872 / *printed*

1377

PARIS, RUE DE CRUSSOL
Manufacture du prince
de Galles
(C. Potter)
1789—1792 / *blue*

1378

FREIWALDAU (Gozdnica)
H. Schmidt
20th cent. / *printed*

1379 

PLANKENHAMMER
Porzellanfabrik
after 1908 / *printed*

1380 

1381 

PRAGUE
K. Kriegel & Co.
after 1837 / *impressed*

1382 

PRAGUE
K. Kriegel & Co.
after 1837 / *impressed*

1383 

CHODAU (Chodov)
Portheim & Sohn
c. 1870 / *impressed*

1384 

POTSCHAPPEL
C. Thieme
after 1872 / *blue*

1385 

SORAU (Żary)
C. & E. Carstens
after 1918 / *printed*

1386 

STADTLENGSFELD
Porzellanfabrik A. G.
after 1889 / *printed*

1387 

SCHLACKENWERTH (Ostrov)
Pfeiffer & Löwenstein
1st half of 20th cent. / *printed*

1388 

FRANKENTHAL
P. van Recum
1795 / *blue*

1389 

SEVILLE
"La Cartuja"; de Aponte,
Pickmann & Co.
after 1867 / *printed*

1390

ZWEIBRÜCKEN, GUTENBRUNN
Christian IV of Pfalz-Zweibrücken
1768—1775 / *blue*

1391

LONGTON
Shore & Coggins Ltd
19th cent. / *printed*

1392

ALT-ROHLAU (Stará Role)
A. Nowotny
1838—1884 / *impressed*

1393
1394

LUDWIGSBURG
Fridericus Rex
1806—1816 / *red, gold*

1395

FRANKENTHAL
P. van Recum
1797—1799 / *blue*

1396

RAUENSTEIN
Greiner Bros
after 1783 / *blue*

1397

VOLKSTEDT-RUDOLSTADT
Holzapfel & Greiner
1799—1817 / *blue*

1398

VOLKSTEDT-RUDOLSTADT
Holzapfel & Greiner
1799—1817 / *blue*

1399

GOTHA
W. von Rothberg
1757—1783 / *blue*

1400

GOTHA
C. Schultz, Gabel & Brehm
1783—1805 / *blue*

1401 
1402 

MARSEILLE
J. G. Robert
1773—1793 / *blue, black, red, gold*

1403 

RÖRSTRAND
Porcelain Factory
20th cent. / *blue*

1404 

MILAN
G. Richard
1842—1860 / *blue*

1405 

MILAN
G. Richard
c. 1850 / *blue*

1406 

MILAN
G. Richard
1870 / *blue*

1407 

MILAN
G. Richard
1860—1870 / *blue*

1408 

MILAN
G. Richard
c. 1870 / *blue*

1409 

1410 

SAINT UZE
G. Revol Père & Fils
after 1780 / *blue*

1411 

MITTERTEICH
J. Rieber
after 1868 / *printed*

1412

MITTERTEICH
J. Rieber
after 1868 / *printed*

1413

ROSCHÜTZ
Unger & Schilde
1821 / *printed*

1414

ROSCHÜTZ
Unger & Schilde and successors
20th cent. / *printed*

1415

SCHMIEDEBERG (Kowary)
Pohl Bros
after 1871 / *printed*

1416

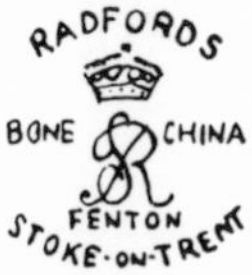

FENTON
S. Radford Ltd
after 1883 / *printed*

1417

FENTON
S. Radford Ltd
after 1883 / *printed*

1418

LONGTON
Hall Bros Ltd
after 1947 / *printed*

1419

SELB
Rosenthal A. G.
1891—1907 / *printed*

1420 

STOKE-ON-TRENT
Mintons & Hollins
1867 / *printed*

1421 

TURIN
G. G. Rosetti
after 1742 / *blue*

1422
1423 

SÈVRES
First Republic period
1793—1800 / *blue*

1424 

FRANKENTHAL
J. N. van Recum
1797—1799 / *blue*

1425 

CHODAU (Chodov)
Richter, Falke & Hahn
after 1882 / *printed*

1426 

CHODAU (Chodov)
Richter, Falke & Hahn
1918—1945 / *printed*

1427 

CHODAU (Chodov)
Richter, Falke & Hahn
1918—1945 / *printed*

1428 

LA MONCLOA
Ferdinand VII of Spain
1817—1850 / *blue*

1429 

EISENBERG
F. A. Reinecke
after 1796 / *blue*

1430 R-g

GOTHA
C. Schultz & Co.
1783—1805 / *blue*

1431 G. R.

MILAN
G. Richard
1860 / *blue*

1432 G. R
1433 R.

MILAN
G. Richard
1842 / *blue*

1434

DOCCIA
G. Richard
after 1896 / *printed*

1435 R/n

RAUENSTEIN
Greiner Bros
1783—19th cent. / *blue, impressed*

1436 G. RICHARD SON
BARONA

MILAN
G. Richard
1847 / *printed*

1437 JULIUS RICHARD & C
S. CRISTOFORO

MILAN
G. Richard
1850—1860 / *printed*

1438

MILAN
G. Richard
1885 / *printed*

1439

MILAN
G. Richard
1868—1881 / *printed*

1440

MILAN
G. Richard
1883 / *printed*

1441 

SHELTON
J. & W. Ridgeway
after 1853 / *printed*

1442 

GRÜNLAS
R. Kampf
after 1911 / *printed*

1443 

SELB
L. Hutschenreuther
after 1856 / *printed*

1444 

RAUENSTEIN
Greiner Bros
1800—1850 / *blue*

1445 

RAUENSTEIN
Greiner Bros
after 1850 / *blue*

1446 

ALT-ROHLAU (Stará Role)
A. Nowotny
1838—1884 / *printed*

1447 

ALT-ROHLAU (Stará Role)
A. Nowotny
1838—1884 / *impressed*

1448 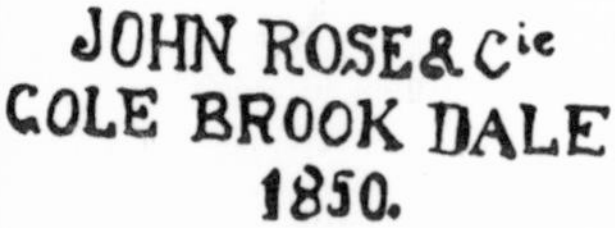

COALPORT
J. Rose & Co.
c. 1850 / *printed*

1449 

SELB
Rosenthal A. G.
after 1908 / *printed*

1450 

KRONACH
Rosenthal & Co.
1933—1953 / *printed*

1451

SELB
Rosenthal A. G.
after 1867 / *printed*

1452

ROSSLAU
H. Schomburg & Söhne
19th cent. / *printed*

1453

RÖRSTRAND
Duke Charles
after 1809 / *blue*

1454

RÖRSTRAND
Porcelain Factory
1838—1840 / *impressed*

1455

RÖRSTRAND
Porcelain Factory
mid-19th cent. / *printed*

1456

RÖRSTRAND
Porcelain Factory
1852 / *blue, gold*

1457

RÖRSTRAND
Porcelain Factory
1857—1860 / *brown*

1458

RÖRSTRAND
Porcelain Factory
from 1870 / *various colours*

1459

GRÜNLAS
R. Kampf
from 1911 / *printed*

1460

MANNHEIM
Rheinische Porzellanfabrik .
after 1910 / *printed*

1461
1462

SUHL
E. Schlegelmilch
after 1861 / *printed*

1463
1464

TILLOWITZ (Tulowice)
R. Schlegelmilch
after 1869 / *printed*

1465

FENTON
S. Radford Ltd
after 1883 / *printed*

1466

TURIN
G. G. Rosetti
mid-18th cent. / *blue*

1467

SCHORNDORF
C. M. Bauer & Pfeiffer
1904 / *printed*

1468

ROYAL-STONE
G. RICHARD & C.

MILAN
G. Richard
1870—1873 / *printed*

1469 

ROZENBURG
Porcelain Factory
1885—1905 / *printed*

1470
1471 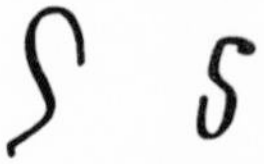

SCHLAGGENWALD (Slavkov)
J. J. Paulus — L. Greiner
1793—1812 / *blue*

1472 

SCHLAGGENWALD (Slavkov)
J. J. Lippert & V. Haas
1810—1820 / *gold*

1473 

SCHLAGGENWALD (Slavkov)
J. J. Lippert & V. Haas
1810—1820 / *blue*

1474 

SCHLAGGENWALD (Slavkov)
J. J. Lippert & V. Haas
1810—1820 / *impressed*

1475
1476 

PARIS, RUE DE LA ROQUETTE
Souroux
after 1773 / *blue, red*

1477 

CAUGHLEY
T. Turner
after 1783 / *blue*

1478
1479 

SCHNEY
E. Liebmann
after 1800 / *blue*

1480 

SCHEIBE-ALSBACH
A. W. F. Kister
after 1834 / *blue*

1481 

SAINT VALLIER
M. Montagne
after 1830 / *printed*

1482

GOTHA
Simson Bros
after 1883 / *printed*

1483

KÖPPELSDORF-NORD
Swaine & Co.
after 1854 / *printed*

1484

SITZENDORF
Voigt Bros
after 1856 / *printed*

1485

SELB
Staatliche Porzellanmanufaktur
Berlin
after 1763 / *blue*

1486
1487

TIEFENFURTH (Parowa)
P. Donath
after 1883 / *printed*

1488

SAINT AMAND LES EAUX
J. B. Fauquez
end of 18th cent. / *blue*

1489

LONGTON
Salisbury China
end of 19th cent. / *printed*

1490

LONGTON
Salopian Warehouse
after 1783 / *printed*

1491

CAUGHLEY
T. Turner, Salopian China
after 1783 / *printed*

1492

SARGADELOS
L. de la Riva & Co.
after 1867 / *printed*

1493

FRAUREUTH
Porzellanfabrik
after 1866 / *printed*

1494

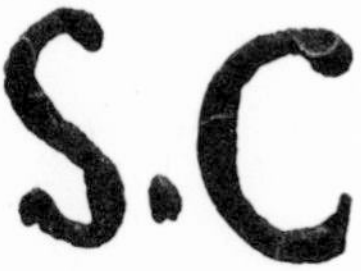

SAINT CLOUD
P. Chicaneau
c. 1677 / *blue*

1495
1496

SCHWARZENBACH
O. Schaller & Co.
after 1882 / *printed*

1497

ARZBERG
C. Schumann
after 1881 / *printed*

1498

SCHWARZENHAMMER
Schumann & Schreider
after 1905 / *printed*

1499

WALLENDORF
H. Schaubach
after 1926 / *printed*

1500
1501

SCHIRNDING
Porzellanfabrik
after 1907 / *printed*

1502

SCHIRNDING
Porzellanfabrik
after 1907 / *printed*

1503

SCHLAGGENWALD (Slavkov)
J. Lippert & A. Haas
1830—1846 / *printed*

1504

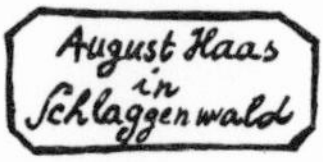

SCHLAGGENWALD (Slavkov)
A. Haas
1843—1867 / *printed*

1505

SCHLAGGENWALD (Slavkov)
Haas & Czjizek
after 1867 / *printed*

1506

SCHLAGGENWALD (Slavkov)
J. Lippert & A. Haas
1830—1846 / *impressed*

1507

SCHLAGGENWALD (Slavkov)
Haas & Czjizek
1918—1938 / *printed*

1508
1509

SCHLAGGENWALD (Slavkov)
Haas & Czjizek
20th cent. / *printed*

1510

SCHLAGGENWALD (Slavkov)
Haas & Czjizek
20th cent. / *printed*

1511

SCHLACKENWERTH (Ostrov)
Pfeiffer & Löwenstein
20th cent. / *printed*

1512

LANGEWIESEN
O. Schlegelmilch
after 1892 / *printed*

1513

SCHLOTTENHOF
Porzellanfabrik
after 1893 / *printed*

1514

PARIS, RUE DU FAUBOURG
SAINT DENIS
Soelcher
1800—1828 / *red*

1515
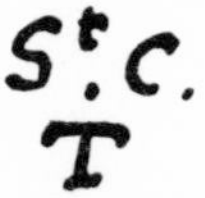

SAINT CLOUD
H. & G. Trou
1722—1766 / *blue*

1516

ARZBERG
C. Schumann
after 1881 / *printed*

1517

SCHWARZENHAMMER
Schumann & Schreider
after 1905 / *printed*

1518

WEISSWASSER
A. Schwaig
after 1895 / *printed*

1519

KÖPPELSDORF-NORD
Schoenau Bros, Swaine & Co.
after 1854 / *printed*

1520

MILAN
G. Richard
1874 / *printed*

1521

SELB
Gräf & Krippner
c. 1900 / *printed*

1522

SELB
Gräf & Krippner
c. 1900 / *printed*

1523

SELB
Heinrich & Co.
after 1896 / *printed*

1524

SELB
Heinrich & Co.
1904 / *printed*

1525

SELB
Heinrich & Co.
1911 / *printed*

1526

SELB
Heinrich & Co.
1905 / *printed*

1527

SELB
Heinrich & Co.
1914 / *printed*

1528

SELB
P. Müller
1928—1943 / *printed*

1529

SELB
L. Hutschenreuther
1858—1920 / *printed*

1530

SELB
P. Müller
1912—1924 / *printed*

1531

MITTERTEICH
J. Richter & Co.
20th cent. / *printed*

1532

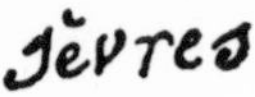

SÈVRES
period of the Consulate
1803—1804 / *gold, various colours*

1533

BOCK-WALLENDORF
Fasold & Stauch
after 1903 / *printed*

1534

FREIWALDAU (Gozdnica)
H. Schmidt
20th cent. / *blue*

1535

LONGTON
Shelley Potteries
1867 / *printed*

1536
1537

KÖNIGSZELT (Jaworzyna Śląska)
Porzellanfabrik
after 1860 / *printed*

1538

TIEFENFURTH (Parowa)
K. Steinmann G. m. b. H.
after 1883 / *printed*

1539

SELB
Krautheim & Adelberg
G. m. b. H.
after 1884 / *printed*

1540

SCHLAGGENWALD (Slavkov)
Sommer & Matschak
after 1904 / *printed*

1541

LANGEWIESEN
O. Schlegelmilch
after 1892 / *printed*

1542

SOPHIENTHAL
Thomas & Co.
after 1928 / *printed*

1543

SORAU (Żary)
C. & E. Carstens
after 1918 / *printed*

1544

SCHELTEN (Šelty)
J. Palme
after 1829 / *blue, impressed*

1545

SELB
P. Müller
after 1890 / *blue*

1546

SPECHTSBRUNN
Porzellanfabrik
after 1911 / *printed*

1547 1548	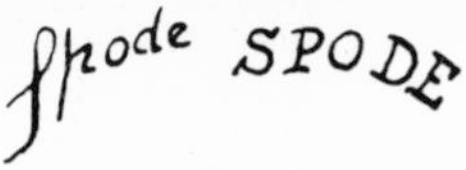	STOKE-ON-TRENT J. Spode *c.* 1790 / *printed*
1549		STOKE-ON-TRENT J. Spode *c.* 1800 / *printed*
1550		STOKE-ON-TRENT J. Spode 1800—1833 / *printed*
1551		STOKE-ON-TRENT J. Spode 1800—1833 / *printed*
1552	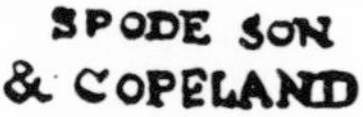	STOKE-ON-TRENT J. Spode *c.* 1833 / *printed*
1553		KRONACH Stockhardt & Schmidt-Eckert after 1912 / *printed*
1554		SAINT CLOUD P. Chicaneau *c.* 1677 / *blue*
1555		PARIS RUE SAINT MERRY Stone, Coquerel & Legros 1807—1849 / *blue*
1556 1557		STANOWITZ (Strzegom) C. Walter & Co. after 1873 / *blue*
1558		FENTON Crown Staffordshire China after 1808 / *printed*

1559

FENTON
A. Bowker
19th cent. / *printed*

1560

FENTON
Crown Staffordshire China
19th cent. / *printed*

1561

FENTON
Crown Staffordshire China
20th cent. / *printed*

1562

LONGTON
Royal Staffordshire China
after 1843 / *printed*

1563

LONGTON
T. Poole & Gladstone
after 1843 / *printed*

1564

LONGTON
Chapmans Ltd
after 1916 / *printed*

1565
1566

LONGTON
C. Amison & Co.
after 1875 / *printed*
c. 1900 / *printed*

1567

TIEFENFURTH (Parowa)
C. H. Tupack
after 1802 / *printed*

1568

SAARGEMÜND
Utzschneider & Co.
after 1775 / *blue*

1569
1570
1571

SUHL
E. Schlegelmilch
after 1861 / *blue*

1572
1573

LIMOGES
Porcelaine de Casseaux
20th cent. / *printed*

1574

SCHWARZA-SAALBAHN
E. & A. Müller
after 1890 / *printed*

1575

KÖPPELSDORF-NORD
Schoenau Bros, Swaine & Co.
after 1854 / *printed*

1576

SWANSEA
L. W. Dillwyn
1814—1830 / *impressed*

1577

SWANSEA
L. W. Dillwyn
1814—1830 / *blue*

1578

SWANSEA
L. W. Dillwyn
1814—1870 / *blue*

1579

RUDOLSTADT
L. Straus & Söhne
after 1882 / *printed*

1580
1581

SCHWARZENHAMMER
Schumann & Schreider
after 1905 / *printed*

1582

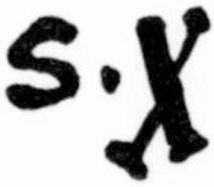

SCEAUX
De Bey, J. Chapelle
1763—1795 / *incised*

1583

LONGTON
J. Shaw & Sons
20th cent. / *printed*

1584
1585
1586

TETTAU
G. C. Greiner
after 1794 / *blue*

1587

TETTAU
G. C. Greiner
after 1794 / *blue*

1588

ZWICKAU
C. Fischer
after 1850 / *blue*

1589
1590

TANNAWA (Ždanov)
F. J. Mayer
1840—1880 / *impressed*

1591

FRANKENTHAL
Carl Theodor von der Pfalz
1762—1797 / *blue*

1592

FRANKENTHAL
A. Bergdoll
1762—1775 / *blue*

1593
1594

FRANKENTHAL
Carl Theodor von der Pfalz
1770—1789 / *blue*

1595

VOLKSTEDT-RUDOLSTADT
Porzellanfabrik
20th cent. / *printed*

1596

WALDENBURG (Walbrzych)
C. Tielsch
after 1895 / *printed*

1597

LUNÉVILLE
P. L. Cyfflé; "Terre de Lorraine"
end of 18th cent. / *blue*

1598

TETTAU
Königliche Porzellanfabrik
after 1885 / *printed*

1599

TETTAU
Königliche Porzellanfabrik
after 1885 / *printed*

1600

TETTAU
Gerold & Co.
after 1904 / *printed*

1601

TETTAU
Gerold & Co.
after 1904 / *printed*

1602

TETTAU
Gerold & Co.
after 1904 / *printed*

1603

LIMOGES
C. Tharaud
after 1919 / *printed*

1604

MARKTREDWITZ
F. Thomas
1903—1908 / *printed*

1605

TILLOWITZ (Tulowice)
R. Schlegelmilch
after 1869 / *printed*

1606
1607
1608

KLÖSTERLE (Klášterec)
Gräfliche Thun'sche
Porzellanfabrik
1804—1830 / *blue, gold*

1609

KLÖSTERLE (Klášterec)
Gräfliche Thun'sche
Porzellanfabrik
1830—1893 / *impressed*

1610

KLÖSTERLE (Klášterec)
Gräfliche Thun'sche
Porzellanfabrik
after 1893 / *printed*

1611

ZWICKAU
C. Fischer
after 1850 / *blue*

1612

TOMASZÓW
F. Mezer
1806 / *blue*

1613

TOMASZÓW
F. Mezer
1808 / *black*

1614

TOMASZÓW
F. Mezer
1808 / *black*

1615

TOMASZÓW
F. Mezer
1806—1827 / *gold*

1616

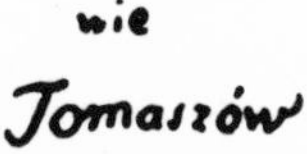

TOMASZÓW
F. Mezer
1806—1827 / *gold*

1617

TETTAU
Gerold & Co.
after 1904 / *printed*

1618

POTSCHAPPEL
C. Thieme
1872 / *blue*

1619

TIEFENFURTH (Parowa)
P. Donath
after 1883 / *blue*

1620

LONGTON
Trentham Bone China Ltd
20th cent. / *printed*

1621

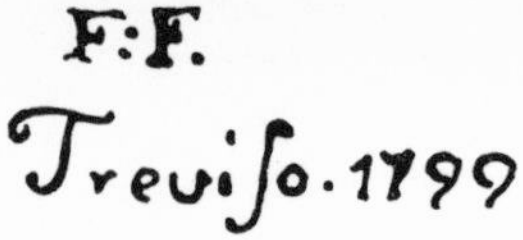

TREVISO
Fontebasso Bros
1799 / *blue*

1622
1623

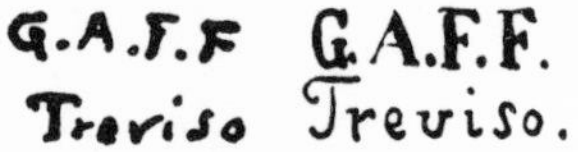

TREVISO
Fontebasso Bros
beginning of 19th cent. / *blue*

1624

TRIPTIS
Porzellanfabrik A. G.
after 1891 / *printed*

1625

COALPORT
W. Taylor
c. 1820 / *blue*

1626

POTSCHAPPEL
C. Thieme
after 1872 / *blue*

1627

UPPSALA
Ekeby Aktiebolag
from 1918 / *printed*

1628

DALLWITZ (Dalovice)
F. Urfus
1855—1875 / *impressed*

1629

UHLSTÄDT
C. Alberti
after 1837 / *printed*

1630

ULM
J. J. Schmidt
1827—1833 / *blue*

1631 

UNTERKÖDITZ
Möller & Dippe
after 1846 / *printed*

1632 

SAINT UZE
G. Revol Père & Fils
after 1857 / *printed*

1633
1634  

VENICE
N. F. Hewelcke
1761—1763 / *incised, red*

1635 

VINOVO
Dr V. A. Gioanetti
after 1780 / *blue*

1636 

VINOVO
Dr V. A. Gioanetti
after 1780 / *incised*

1637 

VENICE
N. F. Hewelcke
1757—1765 / *red, gold*

1638 

VISTA ALEGRE
J. Ferreira Pinto Basto
1824—1840 / *blue*

1639
1640 

VISTA ALEGRE
J. Ferreira Pinto Basto
after 1840 / *blue*

1641 

BORDEAUX
M. Vanier
1788—1790 / *blue, red, gold*

1642 

SAINT VALLIER
L. Boissonnet
20th cent. / *printed*

1643 

VINOVO
Dr V. A. Gioanetti
c. 1800 / *blue*

1644 

VENICE
F. & G. Vezzi
1720—1727 / *blue*

1645 

VENICE
F. & G. Vezzi
1720—1727 / *blue*

1646 

VENICE
F. & G. Vezzi
1720—1727 / *red, blue, gold*

1647 

VENICE
F. & G. Vezzi
1720—1727 / *blue, incised*

1648 

VENICE
F. & G. Vezzi
1720—1727 / *red, blue, green*

1649 

ILMENAU
Greiner and successors
20th cent. / *printed*

1650 

VENICE
F. & G. Vezzi
1720—1727 / *blue*

1651
1652  

LAVENO
Società Ceramica Italiana
20th. cent. / *printed*

1653
1654 

KLOSTER VESSRA
Porzellanfabrik
1892 / *printed*

1655

VINOVO
Fornari
19th cent. / *blue*

1656
1657

ALT-ROHLAU (Stará Role)
Porzellanfabrik Victoria A. G.
after 1883 / *printed*

1658

HOF MOSCHENDORF
O. Reinecke
after 1878 / *printed*

1659

LONGTON
Cartwright & Edwards Ltd
after 1851 / *printed*

1660

SHELTON
J. & W. Ridgeway
1850—1858 / *printed*

1661
1662

COBRIDGE
Viking Pottery Co.
1936 / *printed*

1663

CHANTILLY
Villers Cotterets
1770—1785 / *blue*

1664

SCHORNDORF
Bauer & Pfeiffer
1904 / *printed*

1665

VISTA ALEGRE
J. Ferreira Pinto Basto
1850 / *blue*

1666

VISTA ALEGRE
J. Ferreira Pinto Basto
20th cent. / *printed*

1667
1668

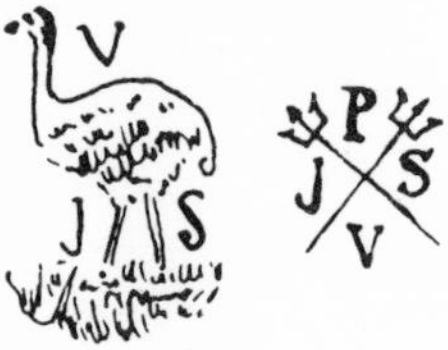

VOHENSTRAUSS
J. Seltmann
after 1901 / *printed*

1669

VOLKSTEDT-RUDOLSTADT
K. Ens
after 1898 / *printed*

1670

VOHENSTRAUSS
J. Seltmann
20th cent. / *printed*

1671

VOLOKITINO
A. Miklaszewski
19th cent. / *red*

1672

CHODAU (Chodov)
Porges von Portheim
after 1845 / *impressed*

1673

VOLKSTEDT-RUDOLSTADT
R. Eckert & Co.
after 1895 / *printed*

1674

FRANKENTHAL
J. N. van Recum
1797—1799 / *blue*

1675

BERLIN
W. C. Wegely
1751—1757 / *blue, impressed, incised*

1676

BERLIN
W. C. Wegely
1751—1757 / *blue, impressed*

1677
1678

WÜRZBURG
C. Geyger
1775—1780 / *impressed*

1679
1680

BORDEAUX
P. & J. Verneuilh
1781—1787 / *blue, gold, red*

1681
1682
1683

WORCESTER
Dr J. Wall
1751—1783 / *blue*

1684

LONGTON HALL
W. Littler
1753—1760 / *blue*

1685

LOWESTOFT
imitations of Worcester porcelain
end of 18th cent. / *blue*

1686
1687

WALLENDORF
J. W. Hamann and G. and J. Greiner
1764—1800 / *blue*

1688

WALLENDORF
J. W. Hamann
1764—1778 / *blue*

1689

WEISSWASSER
A. Schweig
after 1895 / *printed*

1690

VISCHE
L. Birago
1766—1768 / *impressed*

1691

HORN
H. Wehinger & Co.
1905 / *impressed*

1692

WALLENDORF
H. Schaubach
after 1926 / *printed*

1693

WISTRITZ (Bystřice)
Krantzberger, Mayer & Purkert
after 1911 / *printed*

1694

LIPPELSDORF
Wagner & Apel
after 1877 / *printed*

1695

TURN (Trnovany)
E. Wahliss
before 1918 / *printed*

1696

MARKTREDWITZ
F. Neukirchner
after 1916 / *printed*

1697

WALDERSHOF
Porzellanfabrik
1907—1924 / *printed*

1698 

WALDSASSEN
Bareuther
after 1866 / *printed*

1699 

WEINGARTEN
R. Wohlfinger
after 1882 / *printed*

1700
1701

WEIDEN
Bauscher Bros
after 1881 / *printed*

1702 

BLANKENHAIN
C. & A. Carstens
after 1790 / *printed*

1703 

BLANKENHAIN
C. & A. Carstens
after 1790 / *printed*

1704 

WEISSENSTADT
Dürbeck & Rückdäschel
after 1920 / *printed*

1705 

WEISSWASSER
A. Schweig
after 1895 / *printed*

1706 

OESLAU
W. Goebel
after 1879 / *printed*

1707 

ELGERSBURG
E. & F. C. Arnoldi
after 1808 / *blue*

1708 

WALDERSHOF
J. Haviland
after 1907 / *printed*

1709 

VIENNA, AUGARTEN
Porzellanfabrik
after 1922 / *blue*

1710 

WILHELMSBURG
Porzellanfabrik
after 1882 / *printed*

1711 

WEIDEN
C. Seltmann
after 1911 / *printed*

1712 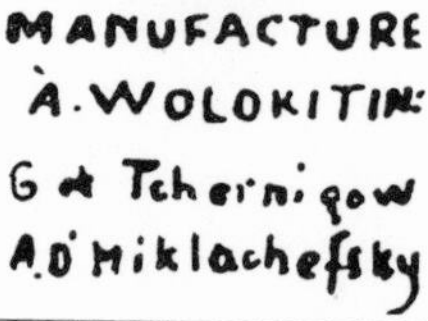

VOLOKITINO
A. Miklaszewski
19th cent. / *red*

1713 

WORCESTER
R. Holdship
1751 / *printed*

1714 

WEINGARTEN
R. Wohlfinger
after 1882 / *printed*

1715 

SCHORNDORF
Porzellanmanufaktur
1904—1939 / *printed*

1716 

LUDWIGSBURG
Wilhelmus Rex
1816—1824 / *red, gold*

1717 
1718 

LONGTON HALL
W. Littler
1751—1753 / *blue*

1719
1720
1721

ZÜRICH
S. Gessner & A. Spengler
1763—1790 / *blue*

1722

ZELL-HARMERSBACH
G. Schmider
1820—1840 / *printed*

1723

REHAU
Zeh, Scherzer & Co.
1880—1930 / *printed*

1724

REHAU
Zeh, Scherzer & Co.
after 1880 / *printed*

1725

REHAU
Zeh, Scherzer & Co.
after 1880 / *printed*

1726

ZELL-HARMERSBACH
J. F. Lenz
1846—1867 / *printed*

1727
1728

ZELL-HARMERSBACH
G. Schmider
19th cent. / *printed*

1729

ZELL-HARMERSBACH
G. Schmider
19th cent. / *printed*

1730

ZELL-HARMERSBACH
J. F. Lenz
1846—1867 / *printed*

1731

OBERHOHNDORF
F. Kaestner
after 1883 / printed

1732

SELB
J. Zeidler & Co.
after 1866 / *impressed*

1733

SEEDORF
Müller & Co.
1907 / *printed*

1734

ALT-ROHLAU (Stará Role)
M. Zdekauer
1918—1938 / *printed*

1735

ZWEIBRÜCKEN, GUTENBRUNN
Christian IV of Pfalz-
Zweibrücken
1767—1775 / *blue*

1736

REHAU
Zeh, Scherzer & Co.
c. 1880 / *printed*

1737

BUDAPEST
Zsolnay
after 1862 / *printed*

1738 

BUDAPEST
Zsolnay
after 1862 / *printed*

1739 

ST PETERSBURG
Imperial Factory, Alexander I
1801—1825 / *blue*

1740 

ST PETERSBURG
Imperial Factory, Alexander II
1855—1881 / *blue*

1741 

ST PETERSBURG
Imperial Factory, Alexander III
1881—1891 / *blue*

1742 

BAKHTEEVO
Count Aksenovich
19th cent. / *blue*

1743 

VOLOKITINO
A. Miklaszewski
1820—1864 / *blue*

1744 

MOSCOW, GORBUNOVO
A. Popov
1830—1872 / *blue*

1745 

MOSCOW, GORBUNOVO
A. Popov
1830—1872 / *blue*

1746 

ARKHANGELSKOE
Prince Yusupov
1827 / *blue*

1747 

ARKHANGELSKOE
Prince Yusupov
1831 / *blue*

1748		BARANOVKA F. Mezer 1828 / *blue*
1749		BARANOVKA F. Mezer 1826 / *blue*
1750		ST PETERSBURG S. Batenin 1812—1832 / *blue*
1751		BARANOVKA M. Gripari after 1895 / *impressed*
1752		FRYAZINO Barmin Bros 1810—1850 / *blue*
1753		FRYAZINO Barmin Bros 1810—1850 / *printed*
1754		FRYAZINO Barmin Bros 1810—1850 / *printed*
1755		MOSCOW, NAROTKAYA Safronov 1830—1840 / *blue*
1756		ST PETERSBURG S. Batenin 1812—1832 / *blue*

1757

BUDY
M. S. Kuznetsov
1887 / *blue, printed*

1758

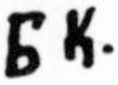

NOVOKHARITINO
T. I. Kuznetsov
after 1800 / *blue*

1759
1760

ST PETERSBURG
Imperial Factory, Catherine the Great
1762—1796 / *blue*

1761

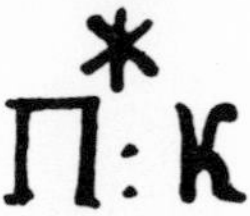

ST PETERSBURG
Catherine the Great, court porcelain
1762—1796 / *blue*

1762

MOSCOW, RYAZAN
J. Gulyn
1830—1850 / *blue*

1763

VERBILKI
F. Gardner
after 1787 / *blue*

1764
1765

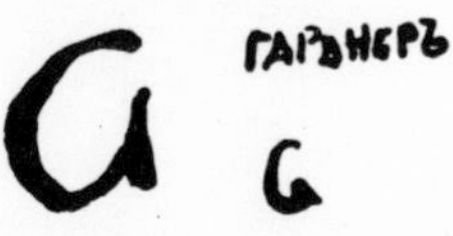

VERBILKI
F. Gardner
after 1787 / *blue*

1766

VERBILKI
F. Gardner
after 1787 / *blue, impressed*

1767

1768

VERBILKI
F. Gardner
after 1787 / *blue, impressed*

1769

GORODNITZA (Horodnica)
W. Rulikowski
1856—1880 / *red*

1770

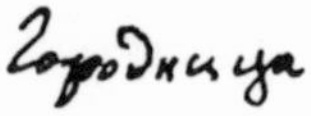

GORODNITZA (Horodnica)
W. Rulikowski
1856—1880 / *red*

1771

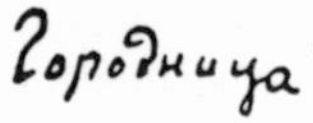

GORODNITZA (Horodnica)
W. Rulikowski
1856—1880 / *red*

1772

GORODNITZA (Horodnica)
W. Rulikowski
1856—1880 / *red*

1773

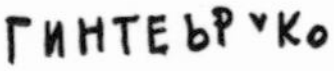

MOSCOW
T. Gunther & Co.
1818—1876 / *printed*

1774

KORZEC
F. Mezer
beginning of 19th cent. / *red*

1775

KORZEC
F. Mezer
beginning of 19th cent. / *red*

1776

ST PETERSBURG
S. V. Kornilov
1835—1885 / *printed*

1777 

1778 

NOVOKHARITINO
Kuznetsov Bros
beginning of 19th cent. / *printed*

1779 

DULEVO
S. T. Kuznetsov
1832 —2nd half of 19th cent.
printed

1780 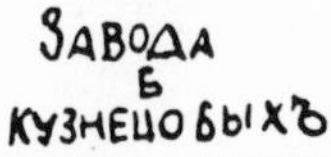

DULEVO
S. T. Kuznetsov
after 1889 / *printed*

1781 

1782 

DULEVO
S. T. Kuznetsov
1832—2nd half of 19th cent.
printed

1783 

RIGA
M. S. Kuznetsov
1842 / *printed*

1784 

RIGA
M. S. Kuznetsov
2nd half of 19th cent. / *printed*

1785 

RIGA
M. S. Kuznetsov
beginning of 20th cent. / *printed*

1786 

1787 

VOLKHOV
I. E. Kuznetsov
1878 / *printed*

1788 

BUDY
M. S. Kuznetsov
1882 / *printed*

1789

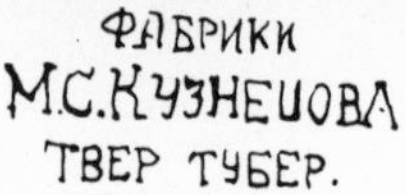

TVER
M. S. Kuznetsov
1891 / *printed*

1790

MORE
C. Golenichev-Kutuzov
1847—1887 / *blue*

1791

ST PETERSBURG
Imperial Factory, Nicholas II
1891 —1917 / *blue*

1792

MOSCOW, SPASSK
D. Nasonov
1811—1813 / *blue*

1793

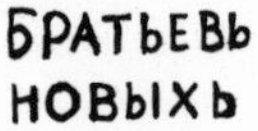

MOSCOW
Novoi Bros
1820—1840 / *printed*

1794

ST PETERSBURG
Imperial Factory, Paul I
1796—1801 / *blue*

1795

ST PETERSBURG
Paul I, court tableware
1796—1801 / *blue*

1796

MOSCOW, GORBUNOVO
A. Popov
after 1872 / *blue*

1797

MOSCOW, GORBUNOVO
A. Popov
1800—1872 / *blue*

1798

VOLOKITINO
A. Miklaszewski
1820—1826 / *blue*

1799

HX

KUSYAEV
N. Khrapunov
1820—1840 / *blue*

1800

LENINGRAD
M. V. Lomonosov Factory 1917
blue

1801

LENINGRAD
M. V. Lomonosov Factory 1917
blue

1802

洪武年製

CHINESE PORCELAIN

A. Reign marks (nien hao) produced during the Hung Wu period
1368—1399 / *blue*

1803

洪武

Hung Wu
1368—1399 / *blue*

1804

永樂年製

produced during the Yung Lo period
1403—1425 / *blue*

1805

Yung Lo
1403—1425 / *blue*

1806

produced during the Yung Lo period
1403—1425 / *printed*

1807

produced during the Hsüan Tê period under the great Ming dynasty
1426—1436 / *blue*

1808
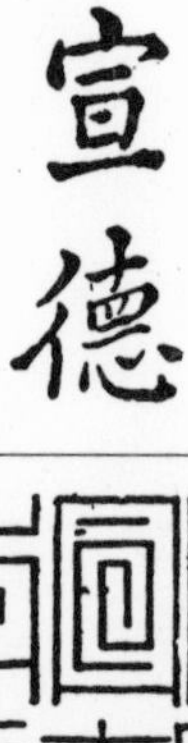
Hsüan Tê
1426—1436 / *blue*

1809

produced during the Hsüan Tê period under the great Ming dynasty
1426—1436 / *printed*

1810

大明成化年製

produced during the Ch'êng Hua period under the great Ming dynasty
1465—1488 / *blue*

1811

成化

Ch'êng Hua
1465—1488 / *blue*

1812

成化年製

produced during the Ch'êng Hua period
1465—1488 / *blue*

1813

produced during the Ch'êng Hua period
1465—1488 / *printed*

1814

大明弘治年製

produced during the Hung Chih period under the great Ming dynasty
1488—1505 / *blue*

1815

弘治

Hung Chih
1488—1505 / *blue*

1816 大明正德年製

produced during the Chêng Tê period under the great Ming dynasty
1506—1522 / *blue*

1817 正德

Chêng Tê
1506—1522 / *blue*

1818 大明嘉靖年製

produced during the Chia Ch'ing period under the great Ming dynasty
1522—1567 / *blue*

1819 嘉靖

Chia Ch'ing
1522—1567 / *blue*

1820 大明隆慶年製

produced during the Lung Ch'ing period under the great Ming dynasty
1567—1573 / *blue*

1821

隆慶

Lung Ch'ing
1567—1573 / *blue*

1822

大明萬曆年製

produced during the Wan Li period under the great Ming dynasty
1573—1620 / *blue*

1823

萬曆

Wan Li
1573—1620 / *blue*

1824

大明天啟年製

produced during the T'ien Ch'i period under the great Ming dynasty
1621—1628 / *blue*

1825

崇禎年製

produced during the Ch'ung Chên period
1628—1643 / *blue*

1826	大清順治年製	produced during the Shun Chih period under the great Ch'ing dynasty 1644—1622 / *blue*
1827	順治	Shun Chih 1644—1662 / *blue*
1828	大清順治年製	produced during the Shun Chih period under the great Ch'ing dynasty 1644—1662 / *printed*
1829	順治	Shun Chih 1644—1662 / *calligraphic*
1830	大清康熙年製	produced during the K'ang Hsi period under the great Ch'ing dynasty 1662—1723 / *blue*
1831	康熙	K'ang Hsi 1662—1723 / *blue*

1832

produced during the K'ang Hsi period under the great Ch'ing dynasty
1662—1723 / *printed*

1833

K'ang Hsi
1662—1723 / *calligraphic*

1834

大清雍
正年製

produced during the Yung Chêng period under the great Ch'ing dynasty
1723—1736 / *blue*

1835

雍
正

Yung Chêng
1723—1736 / *blue*

1836

produced during the Yung Chêng period under the great Ch'ing dynasty
1723—1736 / *printed*

1837

Yung Chêng
1723—1736 / *calligraphic*

1838

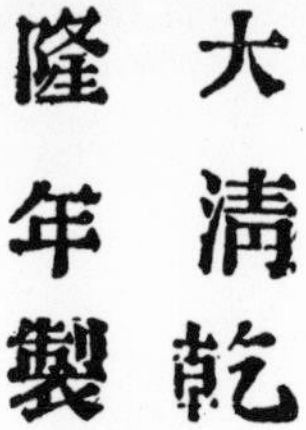

produced during the Ch'ien Lung period under the great Ch'ing dynasty
1736—1796 / *blue*

1839

Ch'ien Lung
1736—1796 / *blue*

1840

produced during the Ch'ien Lung period under the great Ch'ing dynasty
1736—1796 / *printed*

1841

Ch'ien Lung
1736—1796 / *calligraphic*

1842

produced during the Chia Ch'ing period
1796—1821 / *blue*

1843

Chia Ch'ing
1796—1821 / *blue*

1844

produced during the Chia Ch'ing period under the great Ch'ing dynasty
1796—1821 / *printed*

1845

Chia Ch'ing
1796—1821 / *calligraphic*

1846

大清道
光年製

produced during the Tao Kuang period under the great Ch'ing dynasty
1821—1851 / *blue*

1847

道光

Tao Kuang
1821—1851 / blue

1848

produced during the Tao Kuang period under the great Ch'ing dynasty
1821—1851 / *printed*

1849

Tao Kuang
1821—1851 / *calligraphic*

1850	大清咸豐年製	produced during the Hsien Fêng period under the great Ch'ing dynasty 1851—1862 / *blue*
1851	咸豐	Hsien Fêng 1851—1862 / *blue*
1852	大清咸豐年製	produced during the Hsien Fêng period under the great Ch'ing dynasty 1851—1862 / *printed*
1853	咸豐	Hsien Fêng 1851—1862 / *calligraphic*
1854	大清同治年製	produced during the T'ung Chih period under the great Ch'ing dynasty 1862—1875 / *blue*
1855	同治	T'ung Chih 1862—1875

1856

produced during the T'ung Chih period under the great Ch'ing dynasty
1862—1875 / *printed*

1857

T'ung Chih
1862—1875 / *calligraphic*

1858

produced during the Kuang Hsü period under the great Ch'ing dynasty
1875—1908 / *blue*

1859

Kuang Hsü
1875—1908 / *blue*

1860

produced during the Kuang Hsü period under the great Ch'ing dynasty
1875—1908 / *printed*

1861

Kuang Hsü
1875—1908 / *calligraphic*

1862	奇石寶鼎之珍	**B. Hall Marks** Gem among precious wares made of precious stones
1863	奇玉宝鼎之珍	Gem among precious wares made of jade
1864	景濂堂倣古製	produced according to ancient models in Ching-lien Hall
1865	益右堂製	produced in the I-yü Hall
1866	仁和館	Jên-ho-kuan after the year 1000 Sung dynasty
1867	樞府	Shu-fu 2nd half of 13th cent. Yüan dynasty

1868

Beautiful vessel from the Jade Hall
after 1606
Ming dynasty

1869

produced in the Tê-hsing Hall
1573—1620

1870

produced in Fu-kien
Ming dynasty

1871

produced in the Ch'ên-tê Hall
1573—1620

1872

produced in the Chih-lan Pavilion
17th cent.

1873

produced in the Hall of Beautiful Jade in Chü-shun
end of 17th cent.

1874

produced in the Lin-yü Hall
1662—1722

1875

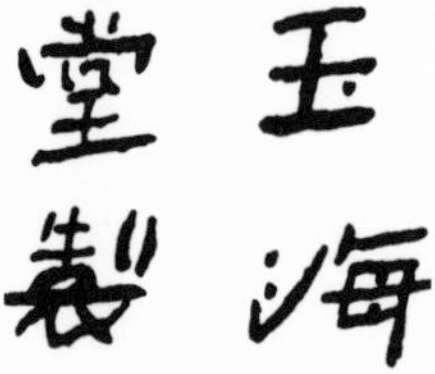

produced in the Yü-hai Hall
beginning of 18th cent.

1876

produced in the Yu-yü Hall
beginning of 18th cent.

1877

produced in the Hall of Precious Jade
beginning of 18th cent.

1878

produced in the Yü-hai Hall
1662—1722

1879

produced in the Yang-ho Hall
1723—1735

1880	澹寧齋製	produced in the Tan-ning-chai Pavilion 1736—1795
1881	敬畏堂製	produced in the Ching-wei Hall 1736—1795
1882	彩潤堂製	produced in the T'sai-jun Hall 1723—1735
1883	彩秀堂製	produced in the T'sai-hsiu Hall 1821—1850
1884	大樹堂製	produced in the Hall of Big Trees 1821—1850
1885	慎德堂博古製	produced in the ancient manner in the Shên-tê Hall 1820—1850

1886	菉猗堂	The Lü-i Hall 18th—19th cent.
1887	大雅齋	The Ta Ya Ch'ai Pavilion *c.* 1900

C. Artists' marks

1888	張家造	made by Chang-chia after 1600
1889	壺隱道人	the Taoist Hu-yin *c.* 1600
1890	王氏寿明	Wang Shou-ming after 1600
1891	建中靖國年製	produced in the first year of the new establishment of the country 1573

1892 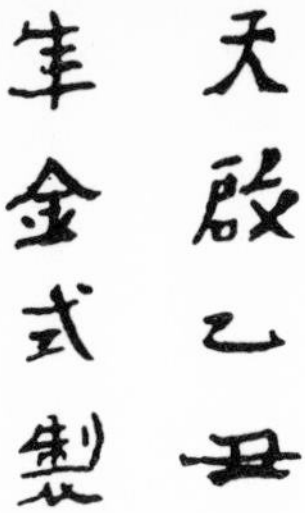

made by Chin-shih in the *i chou* year, during the T'ien Ch'i reign
1597

1893 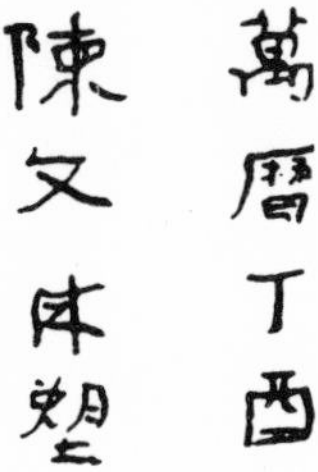

modelled by Ch'en Wen in the *ting yu* year, during the Wan Li reign
17th cent.

1894 

Ch'en-te the Hermit
17th cent.

1895 

Shang-su
1735—1795

1896 

Chung family
13th cent.

1897 

Ch'en-kuo
1662—1722

1898

made by Yüan Hsin-hsing
19th cent.

1899

made by Kung Yüan-chi
c. 1700

1900

made by Ch'en T'ien-sui
1662—1722

1901

made by Sheng-kao in the last day of the fourth month of the third year of the Chia Ch'ing reign
1798

1902

Pai-shih
c. 1724

1903

made by Chiang Ming-hao
1662—1722

1904

Chao-ch'in
beginning of 18th cent.

1905

Lai
1662—1722

1906

made by Liang-chi in the *wu chen* year
1808

1907

made by Chiang Ming-hao
beginning of 18th cent.

1908

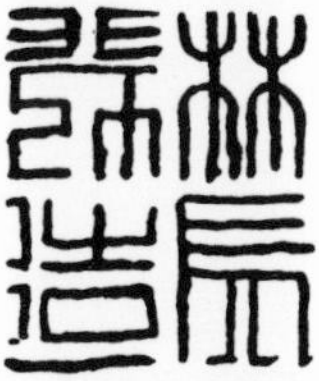

made by Li Chên-fa
beginning of 19th cent.

1909

made by Wang Tso-t'ing
c. 1800

1910 

Lai-kuan
17th cent.

1911 

Yü-chai
c. 1725

1912 

Li-chih
18th cent.

1913 

made by Wang Ping-jun
beginning of 19th cent.

D. Symbolic marks

The eight precious things:

1914 

pearl

1915 

coin

1916 

lozenge (diamond)

1917 

mirror

1918

musical instrument

1919

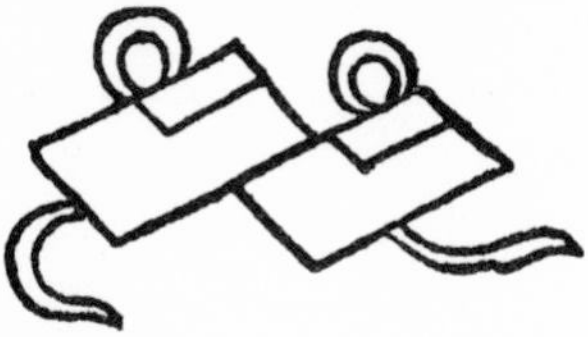

two books

1920

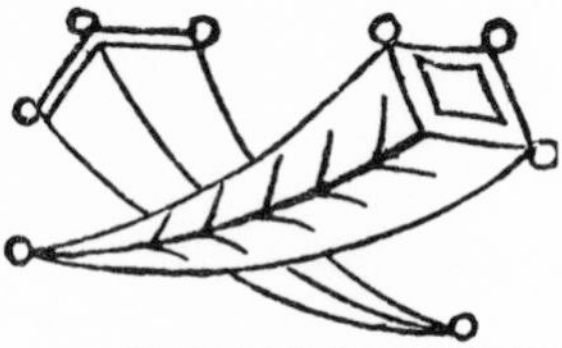

two rhinoceros' horns
(drinking vessels)

1921

leaf of artemisia

The eight Buddhist symbols:

1922

bell

1923

conch-shell (symbol of
a successful day)

1924

umbrella

1925

canopy

1926

lotus flower

1927

vase

1928

fish (symbol of a good marriage)

1929

knot (symbol of longevity)

E. Other symbols

1930

hare (symbol of longevity)

1931

writing implements (symbol of learning)

1932

conch-shell (symbol of a successful day)

1933

leaf

1934

leaf (a different form)

1935

mushroom

1936

mushroom (a different form)

1937

peach and bat (symbol of happiness)

1938

musical instrument

1939

eight-petalled flower

1940

five-petalled flower

1941

bud

1942

four-petalled flower

JAPANESE PORCELAIN

1943

五良大甫
呉祥瑞造

ARITA (Hizen prov.)
Gorodayu Go Shonzui
after 1510

1944

倣余祖先祥瑞
五良大甫所製

ARITA (Hizen prov.)
Shonzui Gorodayu (imitation)
19th cent.

1945

ARITA (Hizen prov.)
Inscription: wealth, honour and everlasting spring
19th cent.

1946

ARITA (Hizen prov.)
Inscription: gem of our precious wares
19th cent.

1947

ARITA (Hizen prov.)
Ya (elegance)
19th cent.

1948

ARITA (Hizen prov.)
Ho (costliness)
19th cent.

1949

ARITA (Hizen prov.)
Fu ku (happiness)
19th cent.

1950

ARITA (Hizen prov.)
Kin (gold)
19th cent.

1951

ARITA (Hizen prov.)
Ka (prosperity)
19th cent.

1952

ARITA (Hizen prov.)
unknown mark
18th cent.

1953

ARITA (Hizen prov.)
unknown mark (a Chinese character)
18th century

1954

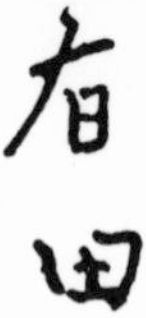

ARITA (Hizen prov.)
Arita (name of city and port)
18th cent.

1955

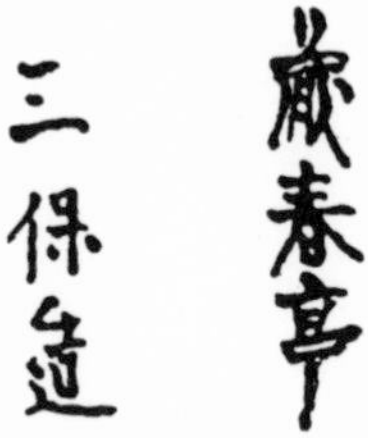

ARITA (Hizen prov.)
Zoshutei sampo (Sampo)
19th cent.

1956

ARITA (Hizen prov.)
Hichozan Shimpo
19th cent.

1957

ARITA (Hizen prov.)
Fukagawa
19th cent.

1958

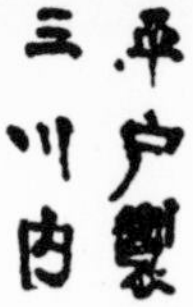

HIRADO (Hizen prov.)
Mikahawacha (factory)
19th cent.

1959

HIRADO (Hizen prov.)
produced in Hirado
19th cent.

1960

NABESHIMA (Hizen prov.)
imitation of old porcelain
from Nabeshima
19th cent.

1961

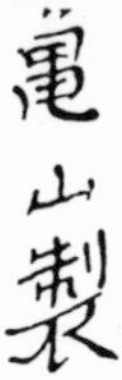

KAMEYAMA (Hizen prov.)
produced in Kameyama
Ist half of 19th cent.

1962

KUTANI (Kaga prov.)
Dosuku (costliness)
18th cent.

1963

KUTANI (Kaga prov.)
place mark
19th cent.

1964

KUTANI (Kaga prov.)
Fu ku (happiness)
19th cent.

1965

KUTANI (Kaga prov.)
Fu ku (happiness)
19th cent.

1966

KUTANI (Kaga prov.)
Sei (produced in Kutani)
19th cent.

1967

KUTANI (Kaga prov.)
city arms
19th cent.

1968

KUTANI (Kaga prov.)
Fu ku (happiness)
19th cent.

1969

KUTANI (Kaga prov.)
Fu ku (happiness)
19th cent.

1970

大日本
九谷造

KUTANI (Kaga prov.)
produced in Kutani, in Great Japan
19th cent.

1971

KUTANI (Kaga prov.)
Tozan (mark representing the clay used)
19th cent.

1972

KUTANI (Kaga prov.)
Ohi (factory mark)
19th cent.

1973

KUTANI (Kaga prov.)
Shiozo (potter)
19th cent.

1974

KUTANI (Kaga prov.)
Fu ku (happiness)
20th cent.

1975

KUTANI (Kaga prov.)
Tozan (mark representing the clay used)
19th cent.

1976

KUTANI (Kaga prov.)
produced by Yeiraku in Kutani
19th cent.

1977

KUTANI (Kaga prov.)
produced by Kioruku in Great Japan
19th cent.

1978

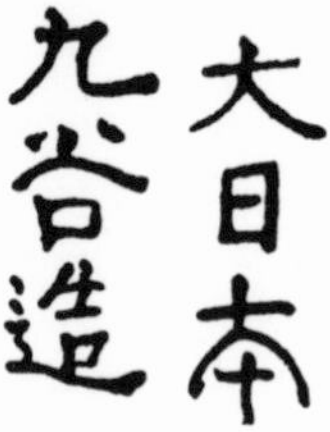

KUTANI (Kaga prov.)
produced in Kutani, in Great Japan
19th cent.

1979

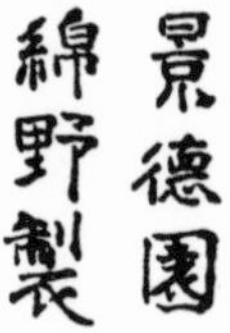

KUTANI (Kaga prov.)
Kichii Watano
20th cent.

1980

HIMEJI (Harima prov.)
produced in Himeji
c. 1826

1981

HIMEJI (Harima prov.)
produced from Tozan clay
20th cent.

1982

SAKURAI (Setsu prov.)
place mark
19th. cent.

1983

OSAKA (Setsu prov.)
Kichiko (potter)
19th cent.

1984

KOBE (Setsu prov.)
place mark
19th cent.

1985

KYOTO (Yamashiro prov.)
place mark
19th cent.

1986

KYOTO (Yamashiro prov.)
Rokubei (potter)
beginning of 19th cent.

1987	大日本 永樂造	YEIRAKU (Yamashiro prov.) produced in Yeiraku beginning of 19th cent.
1988		YEIRAKU (Yamashiro prov.) place mark 19th cent.
1989		YEIRAKU (Yamashiro prov.) place mark 19th cent.
1990		YEIRAKU (Yamashiro prov.) place mark 19th cent.
1991	蘭亭 清玩	RANTEI (Yamashiro prov.) pure jewel from Rantei 19th cent.
1992		RANTEI (Yamashiro prov.) place name 19th cent.

1993

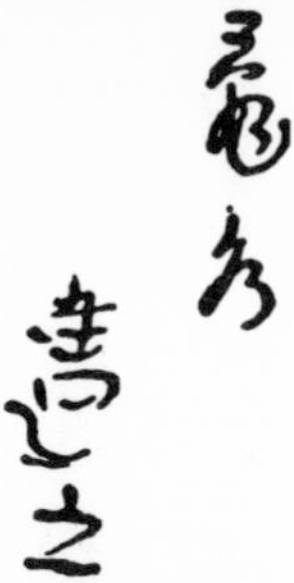

KYOTO (Yamashiro prov.)
produced by Kisui
end of 19th cent.

1994

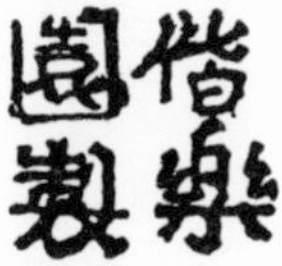

KYOTO (Yamashiro prov.)
produced by Kisui
end of 19th cent.

1995

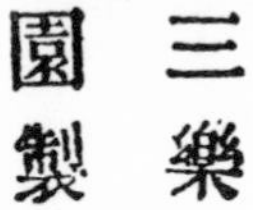

KYOTO (Yamashiro prov.)
produced by Kisui
end of 19th cent.

1996

KYOTO (Yamashiro prov.)
produced by Kiyen
19th cent.

1997

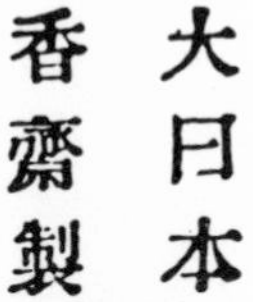

KYOTO (Yamashiro prov.)
produced by Kosai
c. 1856

1998

KYOTO (Yamashiro prov.)
produced by Kosai
c. 1850

1999

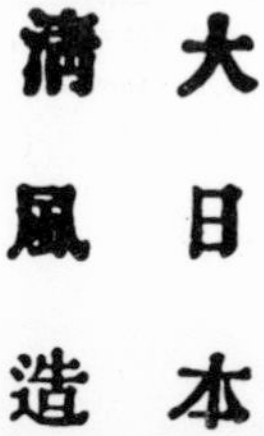

KYOTO (Yamashiro prov.)
produced by Seifu
19th cent.

2000

KYOTO (Yamashiro prov.)
produced by Seifu
19th cent.

2001

KYOTO (Yamashiro prov.)
Ogari Shuhei (potter)
c. 1800

2002

KYOTO (Yamashiro prov.)
produced by Sahei
19th cent.

2003

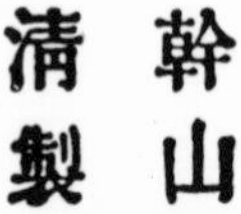

KYOTO (Yamashiro prov.)
carefully produced by Kanzan
19th cent.

2004

KYOTO (Yamashiro prov.)
Kenzan (potter)
19th cent. / *brown*

2005

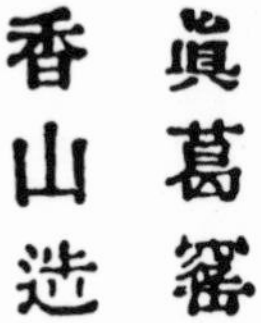

KYOTO
(Yamashiro prov.)
Makuzu Kozan (potter)
2nd half of 19th cent.

2006

KYOTO (Yamashiro prov.)
produced in Gyokusei
2nd half of 19th cent.

2007	嘉永元年 南紀男山製	OTOKOYAMA (Kii prov.) produced in Otokoyama 1848
2008	湖東	KOTO (Omi prov.) place mark 1830—1860
2009	鳴鳳	KOTO (Omi prov.) Meiho (potter) 19th cent.
2010	尾張	OVARI (Ovari prov.) place mark 19th cent.
2011	瀬戸	SETO (Ovari prov.) place mark 19th cent.
2012	大日本 瀬戸製	SETO (Ovari prov.) produced in Seto in Great Japan 19th cent.

2013

SETO (Ovari prov.)
Kato Kanshiro (family of potters)
19th cent.

2014

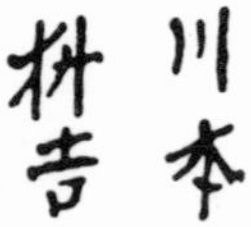

SETO (Ovari prov.)
Kawamoto Masakichi (family of potters)
19th. cent.

2015

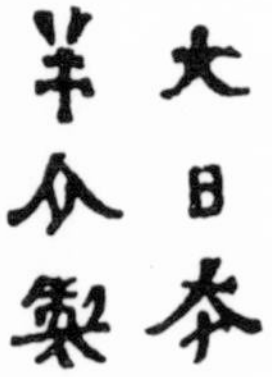

SETO (Ovari prov.)
produced by Hansuke in Great Japan
19th cent.

2016

SETO (Ovari prov.)
tortoise as the mark of local porcelain
19th—20th cent.

2017

七寶會社

NAGOYA (Ovari prov.)
Kaisha (company producing enamel porcelain)
20th cent.

2018

名古屋

NAGOYA (Ovari prov.)
place mark
19th cent.

2019

陶玉園製

TOGYOKU (Mino prov.)
produced in Togyoku
19th cent.

2020

日本美濃國加藤五輔製

TOGYOKU (Mino prov.)
produced by Kato Gosuke in Mino prov.
19th cent.

2021 日本淡路 賀集三平

SAMPEI (Awaji prov.)
Kashu Sampei (place mark)
end of 19th cent.

2022 

SATSUMA (Satsuma prov.)
Hoju (potter)
1780—1800

2023 

SATSUMA (Satsuma prov.)
Hohei (potter)
1820—1840

2024 

SATSUMA (Satsuma prov.)
Seikozan (potter)
1830

2025 

SATSUMA (Satsuma prov.)
place mark
19th cent.

2026 

SATSUMA (Satsuma prov.)
Hoyu (potter)
c. 1840

2027 

SATSUMA (Satsuma prov.)
Hoko or Yoshimitzu
1860

2028

SATSUMA (Satsuma prov.)
mark of the province
19th cent.

2029

SATSUMA (Satsuma prov.)
Same (shark skin glaze)
c. 1888

2030

SATSUMA (Satsuma prov.)
Bekko (turtle shell glaze)
c. 1840

2031

SATSUMA (Satsuma prov.)
Satsu Sei
(produced in Satsuma)
19th cent.

IMITATIONS OF ORIENTAL PORCELAIN MARKS IN EUROPE

2032

MEISSEN
dragon
1723—1733 / *blue*

2033

MEISSEN
Yi-hsing on Böttger's stoneware
1710—1720 / *blue*

2034
2035

MEISSEN
1721—1731 / *blue*

2036
2037

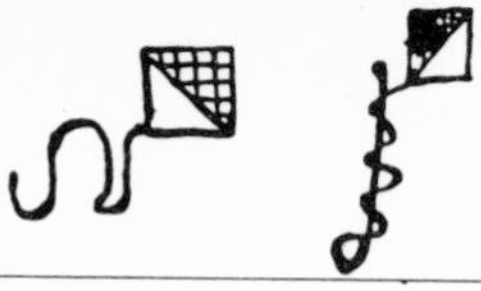

MEISSEN
dragon
1723—1733 / *blue*

2038
2039

MEISSEN
caduceus
1721—1722 / *blue*

2040
2041

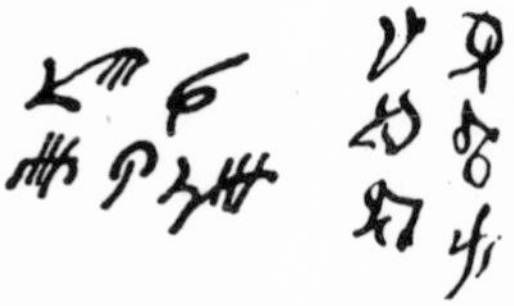

BOW
T. Frye
1755—1760 / *blue*

2042
2043

DERBY
W. Duesbury
1770—1800 / *blue*

2044

DERBY
W. Duesbury
1770—1800 / *blue*

2045

CHELSEA
N. Sprimont & C. Gouyn
1745—1750 / *blue*

2046

CAUGHLEY
T. Turner ("dressed number")
1783—1799 / *blue*

2047
2048
2049

CAUGHLEY
T. Turner
1783—1799 / *blue*

2050
2051

CAUGHLEY
T. Turner
1783—1799 / *blue*

2052

CAUGHLEY
T. Turner
1783—1799 / *blue, red*

2053

WORCESTER
1755—1790 / *blue, red*

2054

PLYMOUTH
W. Cookworthy
1768—1770 / *blue, red,*
incised in gold

2055

STOKE-ON-TRENT
T. Minton
from 1821 / *blue*

2056

RÖRSTRAND
Haancho
after 1884 / *printed*

2057

MITTERTEICH
J. Riber & Co.
after 1888 / *printed*

2058

ANSBACH
Markgräfliche Porzellanmanufaktur
1757—1790 / *blue*

2059

VOLKSTEDT-RUDOLSTADT
R. Eckert & Co.
after 1895 / *printed*

2060

TURN (Trnovany)
Riessner & Kessel
after 1892 / *printed*

2061

ALT-ROHLAU (Stará Role)
Porzellanfabrik Viktoria A. G.
after 1883 / *printed*

BIBLIOGRAPHY

J. F. Blacker, Chats on Oriental China, *London 1908*

M. Brunet, Les marques de Sèvres, *Paris 1953*

W. Burton, and *R. L. Hobson,* Handbook of Marks on Pottery and Porcelain, *London 1909*

W. Chaffers, Collector's Handbook of Marks and Monograms on Pottery and Porcelain, *3rd edition, London 1952*

L. Chroscicki, Porcelana — znaki wytwórni europejskich, *Warsaw 1974*

J. P. Cushion and *W. B. Honey,* Handbook of Pottery and Porcelain Marks, *London 1956*

L. Danckert, Handbuch des europäischen Porzellans, *Munich 1957*

Geoffrey A. Godden, Encyclopaedia of British Pottery and Porcelain Marks, *London 1964*

J. G. Graesse and *E. Jaennicke,* Vollständiges Verzeichnis der auf älterem und neuem Porzellan, Steingut usw. befindlichen Marken. Letzte Neubearbeitung von A. und L. Behse, *22nd edition, Brunswick 1967*

H. Jedding, Europäisches Porzellan, *vol. 1, Munich 1971*

R. M. Kovel and *H. Terry,* Dictionary of Marks. Pottery and Porcelain, *New York 1953*

G. Lukomsky, Russisches Porzellan 1744—1923, *Berlin 1924*

M. Penkala, European Porcelain. A Handbook for the Collector, *London 1947*

E. Poche, Böhmisches Porzellan, *Prague 1956*

R. Rückert, Meissner Porzellan 1710—1810. Katalog der Ausstellung, *Munich 1966*

A. Schönberger, Deutsches Porzellan, *Munich 1949*

M. Swinarski and *L. Chroscicki,* Znaki Porcelany Europejskiej i Polskiej Ceramiki, *Poznań 1949*

C. Jordan Thorn, Handbook of Old Pottery and Porcelain Marks, *New York 1947*

INDEX OF MANUFACTURERS / ARTISTS

Adderley Watership 388—390
Advenir & Lamare 387
Ahrenfeld, C. 565, 566
Aigmont, d' — Desmares 567,568
Aksenovich, count 1742
Albert, R. 564
Alberti, C. 1629
"Alexandra Porcelain-Works" 154, 157
Alexander I 1739
Alexander II 1740
Alexander III 1741
Allen, R. 398—400, 1187
Alluaud, J. F. 1124
Alton China 402
Amison, C. & Co. 1565, 1566
"Amphora" 6
Anchor period 275—7
Anger, A. C. 457
Antonibon, E. P. 26, 27
Antonibon family 535, 1279, 1280, 1302—4, 1308
Antonibon, G. B. 854, 1307
Aponte, de, Pickmann & Co. 1356, 1357, 1389
"Arabia" 145, 158, 443—6, 931, 932, 1333
Aranda, count — Cloostermans, P. 360—2
Arnoldi, E. & F. C. 384, 774, 1707
Aron, M., Père 1217
Artois, Comte d' 654, 655, 1129
Augustus Rex 429—431
Aureaubert, G., d' 1319
Aynsley China 451, 452

Baehr & Proeschild 82, 1317
Baensch, H. 955, 1086, 1087, 1111, 1113, 1114
Baignol, E. 1195, 1196
Balbo, G. 697
Balleroy, H. A., Frères 1130
Balleroy, J. & Co. 1131
Bareuther 1698
Barmin Bros 149, 1752—4
Baroni, G. 1305, 1306, 1309, 1310
Barr, Flight & Barr 523, 524
Barr, M. 467—9
Bartholdi, F. 805, 859
Bauer, C. M. & Pfeiffer 1467
Bauscher, A. 383
Bauscher Bros 440, 1700, 1701
Batenin, S. 1750, 1756
Bauer & Pfeiffer 1076, 1077, 1202, 1206, 1207, 1664
Bayreuther & Co. 488, 514
Beaupoil, marquis de & Co. 1194
Benedikt Bros 528, 1218
Bergdoll, A. 1592
Bernardaux, L. & Co. 1132, 1133
Berthevin, P. 123, 124, 1222—4
Bettignies family 415
Bettignies, M. 453
Beulé, Reboisson & Parot 1134
Beyerlé, J. L. de 536, 537
Bibra, Heinrich III von 809
Billingsley, W. 17
Billingsley, W. & Coke, J. 1328, 1329
Billingsley, W. & Walker, S. 1289, 1290
Bing & Grøndahl 525—7, 661—3, 1031
Birago, L. 1690
Birnay, D. 521
Blancheron, E. 766
Blanka, M. 531

Bloch & Co. 121, 126, 516, 517, 761—3, 771, 772
Bloch Sept Fontaines 1092—5, 1097—9
Bloor, R. 533, 534, 689, 691, 720—2
"Blue Mist" 1240
"Bohemia" 538, 539
Bohne, E. 477, 799
Bohne, E. & Söhne 1285
Boissonnet, L. 1642
Booth & Coclough Ltd 628—630, 1216, 1360
Böttger, J. F. 188, 189
Boussemart, J. F. & Delemer 432—4
Bowker, A. 541, 1559
Brain, E. & Co. 109, 831
Branksome Ceramics 549
Breidenbach, Emmerich von, Kurfürst 290
Bremer & Schmidt 767
Brodel, G. V. 329—331
Broillet, L. 1078
Brow, Westerheat & Co. 558
Brunswick, Carl I of 790—3
Buckauer Porzellanmanufaktur 522
Bühl, H. & Söhne 77, 860, 923

Caluve, J. 570
Carasso, painter 333
Carasso, painter 333
Carstens, C. & A. 177, 1702, 1703
Carstens, C. & E. 592, 1385, 1543
"La Cartuja" 1356, 1357, 1389
Cartwright & Edwards Ltd 543, 777, 1659
Catherine the Great 1759—1761
Cauldon China 571
Ceramica Furga 324, 617
céramique "normande", La 1318
Chamberlain, R. 599, 601
Chamberlains 600, 602—6
Champion, R. 227—231, 335, 336, 550
Chang-chia 1888
Chanou, H. F. 598
Chao-ch'in 1904
Chapmans Ltd 1564
Charey, Sauvageau & Hervé 1327
Charles, Duke 1453
Charles III of Spain 129
Chartres, Louis-Philippe, duc de 1189, 1192
Ch'en-kuo 1897
Ch'êng Hua 1810—3
Chêng Tê 1816, 1817
Ch'en-te the Hermit 1894
Chen T'ien-sui 1900
Ch'en Wen 1893
Chia Ch'ing 1818, 1819,
Chi Ch'ing 1818, 1819, 1842—5, 1901
Chiang Ming-hao 1903, 1907
Chicaneau, P. 425—7, 1494, 1554
Ch'ien Lung 1838—1841
Chin-shih 1892
Ch'ung Chên 1825
Chung family 1896
Coalport China 624—7
Collingwood Bros Ltd 631
Condé, Prince de 297—9, 608
Conta & Böhme 77
Cookworthy, W. 337, 475, 476
Imitations 2054
Copeland, W. T. 632—9
Copeland, W. T., & Garrett 640—8
"Cordoba" 866, 867
Cozzi, G. 273, 274
Cretté, L. 556, 665—8, 1105—9
Crown Porcelain Co. 130—2
Crown Staffordshire China 135, 1558, 1560, 1561
Cuccumos, F. 585
Curtis, J. & M. 1188
Custine, A. P. de 577, 580, 581, 622, 623
Custine, A. P. de — Lanfrey, C. F. 1281, 1299—1301
Cybulski, K. 835, 836
Cyfflé, P. L. 679, 1296, 1597
Czartoryski — Mezer 349, 350

Dahl — Jensens 658
Darte Frères 705, 706
Däuber, F. 419, 421
Davenport 707, 708
De Bey — Chapelle, J. 1582
De Rosly 1374
Delemer 435, 436, 715
Demeuldre, L. — Coché 552—4

Demeuldre, H. 696
Denton China Company 717
Deruelle, P. 322, 323, 711, 712
Deusch & Co. 306
Dietel, J. 1365
Dihl, J. 731
Dihl, J. & Guerhard 1342
Dillwyn, L. W. 737, 1576—8
Dommer, G. & Co. 420
Donath, P. 738, 1486, 1487, 1619
Donovan & Son 739—742
Dorez, F. & B. 529
Dornheim, Koch & Fischer 734—6
Dortu, J. & Müller, F. 114, 115
Doulton & Co. 743—746
Dresden Floral Porcelain Co. 749
Dressel, Kister & Co. 187
Drucko — Lubecki, X. 563
Dubois, J. V. 239, 254
Duesbury, W. 8, 278, 282—5, 348, 363, 470, 687, 688, 690, 719, 725, 726, 753, 972, Imitations 2044
Duesbury, W. & Heath, J. 681—6
Duesbury, W. & Kean, M. 732, 733
Dürbeck & Ruckdäschel 1704
Durham China Company 755

Ehwaldt, J. G., Gottbrecht, J. and successors 847
Eckert, R. & Co. 264—6, 1673, Imitations 2059
Eichler, E. 78, 768, 769
Ekeby Aktiebolag 1627
"Elsa" Porzellan 775
Emanuel, M. & Co. 119, 241, 255, 307
English paint-room of Chinese and European porcelain 515
Ens, K. 778, 779, 1286, 1295, 1669
"Epiag" 86, 780, 781, 1361
Etablissements Demeuldre 555

Fabrique de Monsieur 1210
Fabrique de Porcelaines Blanches & Décorées Anciens Ets. 1155
Fasold & Stauch 133, 1533
Fauquez, J. B. 518, 812, 1488
Fauquez, J. B. & Lamoninary 816, 1079, 1085
"Favorit" 804
Ferdinand IV Rex 838
Ferdinand VII of Spain 1428
Ferreira Pinto Basto, J. 1638—1640, 1665, 1666
Feuillet, J. 798
Fichthorn, J. A. 981
Finney, A. T. & Sons 730
Fischer, A. 391, 392, 1334
Fischer, C. 594, 595, 1588, 1611
Fischer, E. 557
Fischer, F. 813
Fischer & Mieg 178, 827
Fischer & Reichenbach 839
Flight & Barr 709, 823
Flight, Barr & Barr 806, 807, 824
Flight, J. & J. 597, 818—822
Fontanille & Marraud 1135, 1136
Fontebasso, A. & G. 811
Fontebasso Bros 1621—3
Fornari 1655
Frederick Augustus III 803
Fridericus Rex 1393, 1394
Fross Bros 1367
Frye, T. 471,797

Gaignepain, L. F. & Bourgeois, P. 651—3, 713, 714
Galluba & Hofmann 857, 858
Gardner, F. 845, 846, 1763—8
Gareis, Kühnl & Co. 490—2
"Gefle", Porslin 861, 862
Gerarer Porzellanfabrik 883
Gerold & Co. 1600—2, 1617
Gessner, S. & Spengler, A. 1719—1721
Geyer, B. R. 125
Geyger, C. 593, 1677, 1678
Giesche 869
Ginori 25, 853, 873—6
Ginori, C. L. 21—4
Ginori, L. 20
Ginori, R. 311
Ginori — Richard 877
Gioanetti, V. A., Dr 332, 727, 1635, 1636, 1643
Goebel 878
Goebel, W. 19, 120, 1706
Goldschneider, J. 985
Golenichev — Kutuzov, C. 1790
Gorodayu Go Shonzui 1943

Gosse, M. F. 508, 510
Gotha, August von 879
Gotzowsky, J. E. 850, 851
Graf & Krippner 1521, 1522
Gräfliche Thun'sche Porzellanfabrik 1606—1610
Grainger & Co. 885
Grainger, Lee & Co. 886
Greiner & Herda 868
Greiner, F. 814
Greiner, F. C. 55, 56
Greiner, G. 54, 73—5, 1084, 1102, 1103, 1127, 1128, 1169
Greiner, G. C. 92, 1584—7
Greiner, W. 888
Greiner Bros 1396, 1435, 1444, 1445
Greiner family 1121—3
Greiner and successors 1649
Grellet Frères 588—591
Grellet Frères & Massié 828
Gripari, M. 1751
Gronsveldt — Diepenbroek, Count 225
Grossbaum, M. G. 302
Guérin — Pouyat — Elite 1138—1140
Gulyn, J. 1762
Gunther, T. & Co. 1773
Günthersfeld, J. & Co. 79, 852
Günthersfeld, P. 900
Gutherz, O. & E. 1316
Guy, C. B. 1339, 1347

Haancho, Imitations 2056
Haas & Czjizek 34—7, 561, 612—14, 915, 1505, 1507—1510
Haas, A. 912—14, 1504
Hachez, H. & Co. 393
Hachez & Pépin 960
Hadley 917
Haffringue 947
Haidinger, R. E. 439
Haidinger, R. & F. 83, 84
Haidinger Bros 918
Hall Bros Ltd 1418
Hamann, J. W. 1025, 1688
Hamann, J. W. and Greiner, G. and J. 1686, 1687
Hammersley & Co. 919, 1186
Hannong, J. A. 89, 901, 902, 944, 945, 948, 980, 986, 987
Hannong, Paul A. 175, 176, 1350, 1351, 1354, 1355
Hannong, P. A. & La Borde 952—4
Hannong, Pierre A. 267, 268, 903—5, 1352, 1353
Hansuke 2015
Harstall, Adalbert III, von 810
Hasslacher, B. 403
Haviland, J. 921, 1708
Haviland & Co. 926, 1141, 1142
Haward, R. 906, 920
Heber & Co.
Heber & Co. 925
Hébert, F. 249
Heinrich & Co. 927, 1523—7
Heintschel, J. E. 984
Henneberg, E. 848, 849, 880
Hering, J. & Sohn 116, 235, 989, 1037
Hertwig & Co. 102, 1026
Hesse-Darmstadt, Ludwig VIII, of 922, 928
Hesse-Kassel, Friedrich II, of 88, 924
Heubach Bros 5, 69, 312, 908, 943, 1116
Hewelcke, N. F. 1633, 1634, 1637
Hildburghausen, W. E., von 675—7
Hilditsch & Son 969
Höcke, Friedrich 951
Hoffmann Bros 494
Hohei 2023
Hoju 2022
Hoko or Yoshimitzu 2027
Hollins & Warburton 1294
Holdship, R. 1713
Holm, J. J. 956, 958
Holzapfel & Greiner 1397, 1398
Housel & Guy 1340
Hoyu 2026
Hsien Fêng 1850—3
Hsuan Tê 1807—9
Hu — yin, the Taoist 1889
Hudson & Middleton 957
Hughes, E. 946, 1185
Hung Chih 1814, 1815
Hung Wu 1802, 1803
Hutschenreuther 963—5
Hutschenreuther, C. M. 150, 449, 450, 620, 961, 1227
Hutschenreuther, C. M., and

successors 962
Hutschenreuther, H. 959, 1332
Hutschenreuther, L. 970, 1118, 1443, 1529
Hüttner & Co. 560, 728, 1036

Illinger & Co. 1364
"Iris" Porcelain 1000, 1001

Jacquemart, J. 1078
Jaeger & Co. 66, 111, 497, 729
Jäger, W. 773, 982, 983
Johnston, D. 542
Jullien, J. & Jacques, S. 272, 338, 532, 546, 547, 1320

Kaestner, F. 815, 1013, 1731
Kaisha (company producing enamel porcelain) 2017
Kampf, R. 1442, 1459
K'ang Hsi 1830—3
Kanzan 2003
Kato Gosuke 2020
Karlsbader Porzellanfabrik 10017—1022
Karlskrona Porslinfabrik 1023, 1024
Kato Kanshiro (family of potters) 2013
Kawamoto Masakichi (family of potters) 2014
Kenzan 2004
Kerr & Binns 1027
Kestner & Co. 1028
Khrapunov, N. 1799
Kichiko 1983
Kick, E. 416, 417
Kister, A. W. F. 1055, 1055, 1480
Kisui 1993—5
Kiyen 1996
Kling & Co. 301
Knaute, B. 246—8, 530
Knoll, C. 136, 569, 1016
Königliche Hofconditorei Warschau 219, 1029
Kornilov, S. V. 1776
Kosai 1997, 1998
Krantzberger, Mayer & Purkert 1033, 1064, 1693
Krautheim & Adelberg 1062, 1063, 1539
Kretschmann, H. 1012
Kriegel, K. & Co. 1323, 1324
1380—2
Krippner & Gräf 1521, 1522
Krister Porzellanmanufaktur 38, 1051, 1052, 1057—9, 1061, 1065, 1070
Kronester, J. & Co. 495
Krug, Fr. 1011
Krüger, E. 1067, 1068
Kuang Hsu 1858—1861
Kudinov 359
Kuhne, C. 788
Kung Yüan-chi 1899
Kuznetsov 29
Kuznetsov, I. E. 1786, 1787
Kuznetsov, M. S. 1757, 1783—5, 1788, 1789
Kuznetsov, S. T. 1779—1782
Kuznetsov, T. I. 1758
Kuznetsov Bros 1777, 1778

La Borde & Hocquart 456
Lahens & Rateau 1193
Lai 1905
Lai-kuan 1910
Lamoninary 1204, 1205
Lanfrey, C. 618, 619
Lang, A. 395
Lang, F. 458, 459, 817
Lang, J. 992
Lange, H. & Co. 1091
Langlois, W. 509
Lanternier, L. & Co. 1143, 1444
Lassia, J. J. 1080—2
Lauraguais-Brancas, Comte de 472, 1096, 1100, 1101
Lay, J. J. 929
Le Brun, Benoist 1075, 1104, 1191
Leboeuf, A. M. 365
Lehmann, C. A. & Sohn 1115
Lehnert, F. 870, 871
Lenck family 1083
Lenz, J. F. 1726, 1730
Leperre-Durot 117, 118, 1072—4, 1120
Li Chên-fa 1908
Li-chih 1912
Liang-chi 1906
Liebmann, E. 1478, 1479
Lippert, J. & Haas, A. 1117, 1165, 1166, 1503, 1506
Lippert, J. J. & Haas, V. 1472—4
Littler, W. 364, 1684, 1717, 1718

Locker & Co. 723
Lorenz, V. W. 694, 698, 701, 702
Lormello, G. 1203
Lourioux, L. 830, 840, 1184
Lozelet, M. 1197
Lubieński, H., Count 1198—1200
Lung Ch'ing 1820, 1821
Luso Espanola de Porcelanas, Fabrica de Bidosa 1345
Lynker, J. F. & A. 103—106

Macheleid, G. H. 374, 1209
Maier & Co. 770, 1372
Makuzu Kozan 2005
Manka, F. 300
Mann & Porzelius A. G. 95
Manufacture de la Reine Marie Antoinette 381, 382
Manufacture du duc d'Angoulême 855, 856, 1341
Manufacture du duc d'Orléans 1363, 1246
Manufacture Oude Loosdrecht 1251, 1258
Manufacture du Prince de Galles 1377
Manufacture de Porcelaines Ets. Legrand 1168
Manufaktur Porselein Mosa 1268
Manufacture Royale de porcelayne d'Orléans 238
Marseille, A. 413, 414
Martin, C. & Duché 1147, 1148
Martin Bros 1233
Mathes & Ebel 1219—1221
Mayer, F. J. 1589, 1590
Medici, Francesco II 1208
"Medici" porcelain 325
Meiho 2009
Mérault & Petion 1038, 1039, 1325
Merlin-Lemas 1149
Metzel Bros 1232, 1234
Metzler Bros & Ortloff 308, 1245, 1260, 1261
Meyer, S. P. 513, 1269
Mezer, F. 1612—6, 1748, 1749, 1774, 1775
Mezer, M. 30, 460, 461, 478—485, 1009, 1010, 1040—4
Mezer Bros 281
"Mignon" 41, 43, 44
Miklaszewski, A. 1271, 1671, 1712, 1743, 1798
Milde, Ary de 305, 447, 1237
Minton & Boyle 699
Minton, T. 1214, 1215
Imitations 2055
Minton, T., and successors 1238, 1239
Mintons & Hollins 826, 1420
Mintons Ltd 607
Mladenof G. & Co. 540
Möhling, J. 366, 394, 411, 412
Moitte, J. 993, 1211, 1212, 1259
Mol, J. de 1248—1250, 1252—7
Möller & Dippe 1631
Mollert, A. 438
Monier, J. B. & Pellevé, D. 1265, 1266
Montagne, M. 1481
Morgenroth & Co. 881
Mühlhauser, J. P. 864, 865
Müller & Co. 1270, 1733
Müller, E. & A. 664, 1213, 1574
Müller, F. H. 341
Müller, J. N. 995
Müller, P. 498, 804, 1528, 1530, 1545

Nassau - Saarbrücken, Prince of 1314, 1315
Nassonov, D. 907, 1792
Nast, J. N. H. 1291, 1292, 1343
Nathusius 1283, 1284
Neuberg, W., von 872, 1297, 1298
Neukirchner, F. 1696
Neuerer K. G. 1373
New Hall China Factory 1282
Nicolas II. 1791
Nilson, J. O. 916
Nonne, C. 222, 260—3, 973, 974
Nonne, C. & Roesch, K. 245, 1313
Novoi Bros 1793
Nowotny, A. 404, 407, 422, 423, 1312, 1392, 1446, 1447

Oest. Keramik A. G. 81, 108
Ogari Shuhei 2001
Ohme, H. 61
Orléans, Louis Philippe, duc d' 1190
Outrequin, J. B. 1246

Pai-shih 1902
Palme, J. 1335—7, 1544
Paragon China Ltd 28, 1338
Paszoa, J. J. 1090
Paul I 1794, 1795
Paulus, J. J. — Greiner, L. 1470, 1471
Pellevé, D. 765, 789, 1330
Perreira, J. M. 1167
Peterinck, F. J. 234, 315—321
Petion 1326, 1362
Petit, Jacob 994
Pfalz, Carl Theodor von der 1591, 1593, 1594
Pfalz-Zweibrücken, Christian IV of 1735
Pfalzer, Z. 151
Pfeffer, E. 882, 884, 1348
Pfeiffer & Löwenstein 678, 1369, 1370, 1387, 1511
Pillivuyt, C. H. 1358, 1359
Pillivuyt & Co. 1230
Pillivuyt family 829
Planché, A. 718
Plant, R. H. & Co. 1368
Pohl Bros 1331, 1415
Poole, T. & Gladstone 1563
Popov, A. 1744, 1745, 1796, 1797
Porcelaine de Casseaux 1572, 1573
porcelaine limousine, La 1145, 1146
Portheim, Porges von 1672
Portheim & Sohn 1383
Porzelius, A. 428
Porzelius & Mann A. G. 95
Porzellanfabrik "Alp" 1201
Porzellanfabrik Günthersfeld A. G. 1349
Porzellanfabrik Kalk G. m. b. H. 240
Porzellanfabrik Victoria A. G. 863, 1656, 1657; Imitations 2061
Potter, C. 544, 1377
Potter, C. & Blancheron 1344
Pouyat, J. 259, 997, 1126
Prahl, A. F.'s widow 143, 144
Prause, F. 834
Putney & Co. 551

Radford, S., Ltd 1416, 1417, 1465
Raised Anchor Period 286
Raynaud & Co. 1151, 1152
Recum, J. N., van 1424, 1674
Recum, P., van 1388, 1395
Regout, L. & Zonen 1263
Reinecke, F. A. 764, 1429
Reinecke, O. 501, 1264, 1371, 1658
Reinholdt & Schlegelmilch 782
Reinl, H. 966, 967
Retsch & Co. 62, 63, 499
Revol, G., Père & Fils 1409, 1410, 1632
Rheinische Porzellanfabrik 909, 1460
"Rhenania" 695, 756
Riber, J. & Co. Imitations 2057
Richard, A. 437
Richard, G. 1404—8, 1431—4, 1436—1440, 1468, 1520
Richard-Ginori 877
Richard G. & Co. 1005
Richard, S. 1236
Richter, Falke & Hahn 1425—7
Richter, J. & Co. 1531
Ridgeway, J. & W. 975, 1441, 1660
Rieber, J. 1411, 1412
Riemann, A. 649
Riessner & Kessel 6, 367, 418 Imitations 2060
Riva, L., de la & Co. 1492
Robert, J. G. 1401, 1402
Robinson & Son 832
Rokubei 1986
Römer & Födisch 800, 801
Rose, J. 64
Rose, J. & Co. 1448
Rosenthal, A. & Co. 441
Rosenthal, A. G. 1419, 1449, 1451
Rosenthal, P. & Co. 748, 1450
Rosetti, G. G. 1421, 1466
Rothberg, W., von 1399
Rousset & Guillerot 1153
Royal Albert Bone China 396, 397
Royal Crown Porcelain Co. 1110
Royal Rockingham Works 93
Royal Staffordshire China 1562
Royal Worcester Porcelain Co. 134
Rulikowski, W. 1769—1772

Russinger, L. 257, 258

Safronov 1755
Sahei 2002
Salisbury China 1489
Salopian China 1491
Salopian Warehouse 1490
San Cristoforo 80, 596
Schachtel, J. 59, 1003, 1004
Schackert Bros 462, 486
Schaller, O. & Co. 279, 280, 502, 503, 1495, 1496
Schaller, O. & Co. and successors 785—7
Schaubach, H. 968, 1499, 1692
Schierholz, C. G. & Sohn 70—2, 342—4
Schlegelmilch, E. 107, 1461, 1462, 1569—1571
Schlegelmilch, O. 127, 1030, 1089, 1512, 1541
Schlegelmilch, R. 1463, 1464, 1605
Schmerzer & Gericke 303
Schmider, G. 1722, 1727—9
Schmidt, A. 1032
Schmidt, H. 236, 837, 1378, 1534
Schmidt, J. J. 1630
Schneider, J. & Co. 1119
Schoenau Bros 910, 911, 949, 950, 971
Schoenau Bros, Swaine & Co. 269, 1519, 1575
Schomburg, H. & Söhne 1452
Schultz, C., Gabel & Brehm 1400
Schultz, C. & Co. 1430
Schuman, M. & Sohn 1247
Schumann, C. 386, 489, 1497, 1516
Schumann & Schreider 1498, 1517, 1580, 1581
Schwaig, A. 1518, 1689, 1705
Seifu 1999, 2000
Séguin 237
Seikozan 2024
Seltmann, C. 783, 784, 1002, 1711
Seltmann, J. 1667, 1668, 1670
Shang-su 1895
Shaw, J. & Sons 1583
Shelley Potteries 1535
Sheng-kao 1901
Shiozo 1973
Shonzui Gorodayu 1944
Shore & Coggins Ltd 519, 520, 1391
Shun Chih 1826—9
Simson Bros 1482
Società Ceramica Italiana 1651, 1652
Société porcelainière de Limoges 1154
Soelcher 1514
Sommer & Matschak 1540
Souroux 58, 1475, 1476
Spode, J. 1547—1552
Sprimont — Fawkener 275—7
Sprimont, N. & Gouyn, C. 53, 256, 611; Imitations 2045
Springer & Co. 85
Staatliche Porzellanmanufaktur Berlin 1485
Steinmann, K., G. m. b. H. 1069, 1538
Sten, H. 347
Sten, H. and Dortu, J. 1225
Stevenson & Handcock 692
Stevenson, Sharp & Co. 724
Stockhardt & Schmidt-Eckert 1066, 1553
Stone, Coquerel & Legros 1555
Straus, L. & Söhne 1579
Swaine & Co. 1483

Tao Kuang 1846—9
Taylor, W. 1625
"Terre de Lorraine" 1597
Tharaud, C. 1603
Thieme, C. 68, 122, 671, 673, 751, 1375, 1376, 1384, 1618, 1626
Thomas & Co. 511, 512, 1542
Thomas, F. 1604
Tielsch, C. 137, 408, 409, 410, 670, 672, 674, 1596
T'ien Ch'i 1824, 1892
Touze, Lemaître Frères & Blancher 1156
Trentham Bone China 1620
Triangle period 256, 351, 352
Trou, G. & H. 1515
T'ung Chih 1854—7
Tuppack, C. H. 1567
Turner, T. 13—16, 559, 1477, 1491; Imitations 2046—2052

Unger, A. 309

Unger & Schilde 1413
Unger & Schilde and successors 1414
Unger, Schneider, Hutschenreuther & Co. 250—3
Union Céramique 1157, 1158
Union Limousine 1159, 1160
Urfus, F. 1628
Utzschneider & Co. 152, 153, 1568

Vanier, M. 1641
Vaume, J. S. 473, 474
Vermonet, J. & Fils 463—6
Verneuilh & Alluaud 545
Verneuilh, P. & J. 1679, 1680
Vezzi, F. & G. 1644—8, 1650
Vignaud, A. 1161, 1163
Viking Pottery Co. 1661, 1662
Villegoureix 1162, 1164
Villeroy, Duc de 757—760
Villers Cotterets 1663
Voigt Bros 339, 345, 1484
Voigt, H. 67

Wagner & Apel 1694
Wagner, H. 1315
Wahliss, E. 154, 1695
Wan li 1822, 1823
Wanderer, A. C., painter 385
Wang Ping-jun 1913
Wang Shou-ming 1890
Wang Tso-t'ing 1909
"Walküre" 513
Wall, J., Dr 9—11, 232, 243, 353—8, 796, 1681—3
Walter, C. & Co. 1556, 1557
Weatherly & Crowther 242, 244
Weber, M. 96—8, 1006, 1008
Wegely, W. C. 1676
Wehinger, H. & Co. 1691
Weiss, Kühnert & Co. 887
Widera, Dr & Co. 1231
Wilhelmus Rex 1716
Winterling Bros 500
Winterling, H. 493, 504
Wohlfinger, R. 1699, 1714
Württemberg, Carl Eugen of 100, 101, 578, 579, 582—4
Württemberg, Ludwig Eugen, of 1071, 1088

Yü — chai 1911
Yüan Hsin-hsing 1898
Yung Chêng 1834—7
Yung Lo 1804—6
Yusupov, Prince 1746, 1747

Zdekauer, M. 60, 304, 405, 406, 442, 454, 680, 1734
Zeh, Scherzer & Co 39, 159, 160, 505—7, 1723—5, 1736
Zeidler, J. & Co. 1732
Zsolnay 326—8, 1737, 1738

INDEX OF PLACES

Aich (Doubí), CS 366, 394, 411, 412, 457, 780
Alcora, E 360—362
Altenburg, DDR 401
Alt-Haldensleben, DDR 303, 1283, 1284
Alt-Rohlau (Stará Role), CS 60, 300, 304, 403—7, 422, 423, 442, 454, 680, 781, 863, 1119, 1312, 1316, 1392, 1446, 1447, 1656, 1657, 1734
Imitations 2061
Amberg, D 416, 417
Amstel, N 419—421
Ansbach, D 112, 113, 161—3, 368—373, 375—380
Imitations 2058
Arita (Hizen province), J 1943—1957
Arkhangelskoe, SU 1746, 1747
Arnstadt, DDR 270, 271
Arras, F 432—6, 715
Arzberg, D 386, 448—450, 489, 1497, 1516
Augarten *see* Vienna

Baden-Baden, D 151
Bakhteevo, SU 1742
Baranovka, SU 281, 460, 461, 478—485, 1748, 1749, 1751
Barcelona, E 110
Basdorf, DDR 462, 486
Bayreuth, D 385, 513, 981, 1269
Bayswater, GB 515
Belleek, IRL 521
Berlin 179—186, 340, 850, 851, 1050, 1053, 1054, 1060, 1675, 1676
Berlin, Moabit 1247
Blankenhain, DDR 177, 1067, 1068, 1702, 1703
Bock-Wallendorf, DDR 133, 1533
Boisette, F 463—6
Bordeaux, F 542, 545, 1193, 1641, 1679, 1680
Boulogne, F 947
Bourg la Reine, F 338, 532, 546, 547, 1320
Bournemouth, GB 549
Bow, GB 8, 242, 244, 278, 282—285, 348, 363, 470, 471, 797, 844, 972; Imitations 2040, 2041
Božičany *see* Poschetzau
Bristol, GB 227—231, 335, 336, 475, 476, 550, 551
Brussels, B 473, 556, 665—8, 1105—9
Brussels, Etterbeek, B 552—5, 696, 788
Brussels, Schaerbeek, B 474
Březová *see* Pirkenhammer
Budapest, H 557, 1737, 1738
Budau (Budov), CS 395, 458, 459, 817
Budov *see* Budau
Budy, SU 1757, 1788
Buen Retiro, E 47, 49—52, 129
Burslem, GB 743—6
Bystřice *see* Wistritz

Caen, F 567, 568
Canetto sull'Oglio, *see* Mantua
Capodimonte, GB 40, 45, 46, 48
Caughley, GB 13—16, 1477, 1491; Imitations 2046—2052
Chantilly, F 297—9, 608, 1217,

1663
Charlottenbrunn (Zofiówka), PL 59, 1003, 1004
Chatillon, F 609, 610
Chelsea, GB 53, 224, 256, 275—7, 286, 351, 352, 611, 1288; Imitations 2045
Chodau (Chodov), CS 37, 560, 561, 612—4, 728, 1036, 1383, 1425—7, 1672
Chodov *see* Chodau
Chodzież, PL 562, 615, 616
Cluj *see* Klausenburg
Ćmielów, PL 563, 621, 656, 835, 836
Coalbrookdale *see* Coalport
Coalport (Coalbrookdale), GB 64, 572—6, 587, 624—7, 669, 700, 710, 1183, 1293, 1448, 1625
Cobridge, GB 1661, 1662
Coburg, D 649
Copenhagen, DK 18, 31—3, 139—141, 341, 438, 525—7, 657—663, 704, 716, 802, 956, 958, 1031
Creidlitz, D 650, 1346
Crépy en Valois, F 651—3, 713, 714

Dallwitz (Dalovice), CS 694, 698, 701, 702, 813, 842, 1628
Dalovice *see* Dallwitz
Damm, D 292—6, 703
Delft, N 305, 447, 570, 1237
Derby, GB 130—2, 233, 533, 534, 681—692, 718—726, 732, 733, 753, 1110; Imitations 2042—4
Doccia, I 20—5, 311, 853, 873—6, 1278, 1434
Doubí *see* Aich
Dresden, DDR 693, 750, 752
Dubí *see* Eichwald
Dublin, IRL 739—742
Duchcov *see* Dux
Duisdorf, D 695, 756
Dulevo, SU 1779—1782
Dux (Duchcov), CS 78, 768, 769

Eichwald (Dubí), CS 121, 126, 516, 517, 761—3, 771, 772, 1231
Eisenberg, DDR 240, 764, 767, 773, 982, 983, 1015, 1045, 1429
Elbogen (Loket), CS 83—6, 439, 918, 1012
Elgersburg, D 384, 774, 1226, 1707
Ellwangen, D 143, 144
Erbendorf, D 783, 784
Erkersreuth, D 494
Etiolles, F 765, 789, 1265, 1266, 1330

Fenton, GB 109, 135, 541, 831, 832, 946, 1185, 1416, 1417, 1465, 1558—1561
Fischern (Rybáře), CS 136, 569, 1016—1022
Florence, I 325, 1208
Foëcy, F 829, 830, 840, 1184, 1358
Fontainebleau, F 994
Frankenthal, D 89, 175, 176, 980, 986, 987, 1354, 1355, 1388, 1395, 1424, 1591—4, 1674
Fraureuth, DDR 800, 801, 833, 841, 1493
Freiwaldau (Gozdnica), PL 236, 837, 1378, 1534
Fryazino, SU 149, 1752—4
Friedland (Frýdlant), CS 984
Frýdlant *see* Friedland
Fulda, D 334, 809, 810
Fürstenberg, D 94, 790—5

Gateshead, GB 755
Gehren, DDR 79, 852, 900, 1349
Geneva, CH 864, 865
Gera, DDR 847
Gerona, E 866, 867
Giesshübel (Kysibl), CS 245—8, 530, 870—2, 1297, 1298
Gorodnitza (Horodnica), PL 1769—1772
Gozdnica *see* Freiwaldau
Gorbunovo *see* Moscow
Gotha, DDR 848, 849, 879—882, 884, 1348, 1399, 1400, 1430, 1482
Gräfenroda, DDR 734—6
Gräfenthal, DDR 250—3, 887
Grossbreitenbach, DDR 73, 77, 860, 923
Grünlas (Loučky), CS 1442, 1459
Grünstadt, D 805, 859
Gustavsberg, S 424, 889—899

Gutenbrunn *see* Zweibrücken

Hackefors, S 916
Hague, The, N 103—106
Hanley, GB 628—630, 1216, 1240, 1360
Helsinki, SF 145, 158, 443—6, 931, 932, 1333
Herend, H 91, 146—8, 933—942
Hildesheim, D 128
Himeji (Harima province), J 1980, 1981
Hirado (Hizen province), J 1958, 1959
Hlubany *see* Lubau
Höchst, D 287—290
Hof Moschendorf, D 501, 1264, 1371, 1658
Hohenberg, D 150, 620, 961—5, 1227
Horn (Hory), CS 1691
Horodnica *see* Gorodnitza
Hory *see* Horn
Hüttensteinach, DDR 910, 911, 949, 950, 971

Irún, E 1345
Ilmenau, DDR 75, 308, 391, 392, 857, 858, 973, 974, 976—9, 990, 991, 996, 998, 999, 1245, 1260, 1261, 1313, 1334, 1649

Jaworzyna Ślaska *see* Königszelt
Jedlina Zdrój *see* Charlottenbrunn

Kaltenhof (Oblanov), CS 1365
Kahla, DDR 142, 1014, 1115
Kameyama (Hizen province), J 1961
Karlskrona, S 1023
Kassel, D 88, 924
Katzhütte, DDR 102, 1025, 1026
Kelsterbach, D 922, 928—930
Klášterec *see* Klösterle
Klausenburg (Cluj), R 1000, 1001
Kleneč *see* Klentsch
Klentsch (Kleneč), CS 1032
Kloster Veilsdorf, DDR 55, 56, 675—7
Kloster Vessra, DDR 1653, 1654
Klösterle (Klášterec), CS 96—8, 1006—8, 1606—1610
Kobe (Setzu province), J 1984
Königszelt (Jaworzyna Śląska), PL 441, 1034, 1035, 1536, 1537
Könitz, DDR 1232, 1234, 1235
Köppelsdorf, DDR 116, 235, 312, 989, 1037
Köppelsdorf-Nord, DDR 269, 413, 414, 1483, 1519, 1575
Korzec, PL 349, 350, 1009, 1010, 1038—1044, 1325, 1326, 1362, 1774, 1775
Koto (Omi province), J 2008, 2009
Kowary *see* Schmiedeberg
Kronach, D 748, 1066, 1450, 1553
Krummennaab, D 1091, 1364
Kusyaev, SU 1799
Kutani (Kaga province), J 1962—1979
Kyoto (Yamashiro province), J 1985, 1986, 1993—2006
Kysibl *see* Giesshübel

La Moncloa, E 1228, 1229, 1262, 1428
Landstuhl, D 1065
Lane End, GB 969
Langewiesen, DDR 127, 1030, 1089, 1512, 1541
Lassay, F 472, 1096, 1100, 1101
La Seynie, F 1194—6
Lauf, D 1011
Laveno, I 1651, 1652
Leningrad, SU 1800, 1801
Le Nove, I 26, 27, 535, 854, 1279, 1280, 1302—1310
Lettin, DDR 955, 1086, 1087, 1111—14
Lichte, DDR 5, 69, 908, 943, 1116
Lille, F 117, 118, 529, 1072—4, 1120
Limbach, DDR 54, 74, 76, 1084, 1102, 1103, 1121—3, 1127, 1128, 1169
Limoges, F 565, 566, 588—591, 828, 926, 997, 1124—6, 1129—1164, 1168, 1572, 1573, 1603
Lippelsdorf, DDR 1694
Lisbon, P 1090, 1167
Loket *see* Elbogen
Longton, GB 28, 388—390, 396, 397, 402, 451, 452, 519, 520,

543, 631, 717, 730, 749, 754, 777, 919, 957, 1186, 1338, 1368, 1391, 1418, 1489, 1490, 1535, 1562—5, 1568, 1583, 1620, 1659
Longton Hall, GB 364, 1684, 1717, 1718
Lorch, D 306
Lorient, F 1327
Loučky *see* Grünlas
Lowestoft, GB 12, 223, 398—400, 906, 920, 1187, 1188, 1685
Lubartów, PL 1198—1200
Lubau (Hlubany), CS 1233
Lubenz (Žlutice), CS 966, 967
Ludwigsburg, D 99—101, 578, 579, 582—4, 1071, 1088, 1393, 1394, 1716
Lunéville, F 679, 1296, 1597
Luxembourg, L 1092—5, 1097—9

Maastricht, N 1263, 1268
Mäbendorf, DDR 1219—1221
Magdeburg-Buckau, DDR 522
Mannheim, D 909, 1460
Mantua, Canetto sull'Oglio, I 324, 617, 843
Marieberg, S 123, 124, 347, 1222—5
Marktleuthen, D 493, 504
Marktredwitz, D 66, 111, 497, 729, 1604, 1696
Marktschwaben, D 90
Marseille, F 1401, 1402
Mayerhöfen, CS 528, 1218
Mehun sur Yèvre, F 1230, 1359
Meissen, DDR 188—221, 429—431, 803, 1029, 1046—9, 1267, 1287, 2032—9
Mennecy, F 757—760
Merkelsgrün (Merklín), CS 65, 775
Merklín *see* Merkelsgrün
Middleton, GB 776
Milan, I 80, 437, 596, 877, 1005, 1236, 1404—8, 1431—3, 1436—1440, 1468, 1520
Mitterteich, D 119, 241, 255, 307, 496, 1241—3, 1411, 1412, 1531; Imitations 2057
Moabit *see* Berlin
More, SU 1790
Moscow, SU 359, 907, 1773, 1793
Moscow, Gorbunovo, SU 1744, 1745, 1796, 1797
Moscow, Narotkaya, SU 1755
Moscow, Ryazan, SU 1762
Moscow, Spassk, SU 1792

Nabeshima (Hizen province), J 1960
Nagoya (Ovari province), J 2017, 2018
Nantgarw, GB 1289, 1290
Naples, I
Naples, I 838, 1272—6
Neu-Rohlau (Nová Role), CS 538, 539
Neustadt, DDR 925
New Hall *see* Shelton
Niderviller, F 536, 537, 577, 580, 581, 618, 619, 622, 623, 1281, 1299—1301
Niedersalzbrunn (Szczawienko), PL 61, 834
Nová Role *see* Neu-Rohlau
Novgorod, SU 29
Novi Sad, YU 1311
Novokharitino, SU 1758, 1777, 1778
Nymphenburg, D 170—4
Nyon, CH 114, 115

Oberhohndorf, DDR 815, 1013, 1731
Oberkotzau, D 868, 1373
Oblanov *see* Kaltenhof
Oeslau, D 19, 120, 878, 1706
Ohrdruf, DDR 82, 301, 1028, 1317
Oissel, F 1318
Orléans, F 57, 238, 1075, 1104, 1191, 1319
Osaka (Setsu province), J 1983
Ostrov *see* Schlackenwerth
Otokoyama (Kii province), J 2007
Ottweiler, D 1314, 1315
Oude Loosdrecht, N 1248—1258
Ovari (Ovari province), J 2010

Paris, Barrière de Reuilly, F 598, 1080—2
Paris, Clignancourt, F 322, 323, 711, 712, 993, 1210—2, 1259
Paris, Faubourg Saint Denis, F

267, 268, 654, 655, 905
Paris, Gros Caillou, F 387, 1078
Paris, Pont aux Choux, F 41, 43, 44
Paris, Rue Amelot, F 1190, 1246, 1363
Paris, Rue de Bondy, F 731, 855, 856, 1341, 1342
Paris, Rue de Charonne, F 705, 706
Paris, Rue de Crussol, F 544, 766, 1344, 1377
Paris, Rue du Faubourg Saint Denis, F 1514
Paris, Rue Fontaine au Roy, F 257—9
Paris, Rue de la Paix, F 798
Paris, Rue du Petit Carrousel, F 1339, 1347
Paris, Rue de la Roquette, F 58, 239, 249, 254, 1475, 1476
Paris, Rue Popincourt, F 1291, 1292, 1343
Paris, Rue Saint Merry, F 1555
Paris, Rue Thiroux, F 365, 381, 382, 1340
Parowa *see* Tiefenfurth
Passau, D 187, 291, 1083
Pécs, H 326—8
Pinxton, GB 17, 1328, 1329
Pirkenhammer (Březová), CS 138, 178, 595, 827, 839, 951, 1361
Plankenhammer, D 487, 1367, 1379
Plaue, DDR 70—2, 342—4
Plymouth, GB 337; Imitations 2054
Podbořany *see* Podersam
Podersam (Podbořany), CS 1201
Pontenx, F 1374
Poschetzau (Božičany), CS 770, 1372
Pössneck, DDR 87
Potschappel, DDR 68, 122, 671, 673, 751, 1375, 1376, 1384, 1618, 1626
Prague, CS 1323, 1324, 1380—2
Probstzella, DDR 959, 1332

Rantei (Yamashiro province), J 1991, 1992
Rauenstein, DDR 1396, 1435, 1444, 1445
Rehau, D 39, 159, 160, 505—7, 1723—5, 1736
Reichenstein, DDR 531
Riga, SU 1783—5
Rockingham, GB 548
Rome, I 585
Rörstrand, S 125, 1403, 1453—8 Imitations 2056
Rotschütz, DDR 1413, 1414
Röslau, D 500
Rosslau, DDR 1452
Rozenburg, N 1469
Rudolstadt, DDR 477
Rybáře *see* Fischern

Saargemünd, D 152, 153, 1568
Saint Amand les Eaux, F 415, 453, 518, 812, 1488
Saint Cloud, F 1—3, 42, 425—7, 1494, 1515, 1554
Saint Vallier, F 1481, 1642
Saint Uze, F 1409, 1410, 1632
Sakurai (Setsu province), J 1982
Sampei (Awaji province), J 2021
Sargadelos, E 1492
Satsuma (Satsuma province), J 2022—2031
Sceaux, F 272, 1582
Schaala, DDR 67
Schedewitz, DDR 309
Scheibe-Alsbach, DDR 1055, 1056, 1480
Schelten (Šelty), CS 1335—7, 1544
Schirding, D 7, 1500—2
Schlackenwerth (Ostrov), CS 678, 1369, 1370, 1387, 1511
Slavkov *see* Schlaggenwald
Schlottenhof, D 1513
Schmiedeberg (Kowary), PL 1331, 1415
Schney, D 1478, 1479
Schönwald, D 995
Schorndorf, D 586, 1076, 1077, 1202, 1206, 1207, 1467, 1664, 1715
Schwarza-Saalbahn, DDR 664, 1213, 1574
Schwarzenbach, D 279, 280, 495, 502, 503, 1495, 1496
Schwarzenhammer, D 1498, 1517, 1580, 1581

Seedorf, D 1733
Selb, D 498, 804, 927, 970, 1062, 1063, 1118, 1419, 1443, 1449, 1451, 1485, 1521—1530, 1539, 1545, 1732
Śelty *see* Schelten
Seto (Ovari province), J 2011—16
Seville, E 1356, 1357, 1389
Sèvres, F 1180—2, 1244, 1277, 1422, 1423, 1532
Shelton, GB 558, 571, 975, 1441, 1660
Shelton, New Hall, GB 1282, 1294
Sitzendorf, DDR 339, 345, 1484
Sitzerode, DDR 374
Schlaggenwald (Slavkov), CS 34—6, 912—5, 1117, 1165, 1166, 1470—4, 1503—1510, 1540
Sophienthal, D 511, 512, 1542
Sorau (Żary), PL 592, 1385 1543
Spechtsbrunn, DDR 1546
St Petersburg, SU 1739—1741, 1750, 1756, 1759—1761, 1776, 1791, 1794, 1795
Stadtlengsfeld, DDR 310, 313, 787, 808, 1366, 1386
Stanowitz (Strzegom), PL 1556, 1557
Stará Role *see* Alt Rohlau
Stoke-on-Trent, GB 607, 632—648, 699, 826, 1214, 1215, 1238, 1239, 1420, 1547—1552
Imitations 2055
Strasbourg, F 901—4, 944, 945, 948, 988, 1350—3
Suhl, DDR 107, 1461, 1462, 1569—1571
Swansea, GB 737, 1556—8
Swinton, GB 93, 548
Szczawienko *see* Niedersalzbrunn

Tanawa (Ždanov), CS 1589, 1590
Tettau, D 92, 1584—7, 1598—1602, 1617
Tiefenfurth (Parowa), PL 738, 1069, 1486, 1487, 1538, 1567, 1619
Tillowitz (Tulowice), PL 782, 1463, 1464, 1605
Tirschenreuth, D 155, 156
Togyoku (Mino province), J 2019, 2020
Tomaszów, PL 30, 1612—16
Tournai, B 234, 314—321
Treviso, I 811, 1621—3
Triptis, DDR 1321, 1322, 1624
Trnovany *see* Turn
Tulowice *see* Tillowitz
Turin, I 1421, 1466
Turn (Trnovany), CS 6, 154, 157, 367, 418, 1695
Imitations 2060
Tver, SU 1789

Uhlstädt, DDR 564, 1629
Ulm, D 1630
Unterköditz, DDR 1631
Untermhaus, DDR 883
Unterweissbach, A 95, 428, 968
Uppsala, S 861, 862, 1024, 1627

Valenciennes, F 816, 1079, 1085, 1204, 1205
Valognes—Bayeux, F 508—510
Vaux, F 456
Vendrennes, F 1197
Venice, I 273, 274, 1633, 1634, 1637, 1644—8, 1650
Verbilki, SU 845, 846, 1763—8
Vienna, A 164—9, 302, 540, 985
Vienna, Augarten, A 455, 1709
Vienna, Wilhelmsburg, A 81, 108
Vierzon, F 393, 960
Villedieu sur Indre, F 992
Vincennes, F 237, 952—4, 1170—9, 1189, 1192
Vinovo, I 329—33, 697, 727, 1203, 1635, 1636, 1643, 1655
Vische, I 1690
Vista Alegre, P 1638—1640, 1665, 1666
Vohenstrauss, D 1002, 1667, 1668, 1670
Volkhov, SU 1786, 1787
Volkstedt — Rudolstadt, DDR 4 222, 260—6, 778, 779, 799, 814 888, 1209, 1270, 1285, 1286 1295, 1397, 1398, 1579, 1595 1669, 1673; Imitations 2059
Volokitino, SU 1271, 1671, 1712 1743, 1798

Walbrzych *see* Waldenburg
Waldenburg (Walbrzych), PL 38, 137, 408, 410, 670, 672, 674, 1051, 1052, 1057—9, 1061, 1070, 1596
Waldershof, D 921, 1697, 1708
Waldsassen, D 488, 490—2, 514, 1698
Wallendorf, DDR 1499, 1686—8 1692
Weesp, N 225, 226
Weiden, D 383, 440, 1700, 1701 1711
Weingarten, D 1699, 1714
Weissenstadt, D 1704
Weisswasser, DDR 1518, 1689, 1705
Wilhelmsburg, A 825, 1710
Wilhelmsburg *see also* Vienna
Windisch-Eschenbach, D 785, 786, 787
Wistritz (Bystřice), ČS 1033, 1064, 1693
Worcester, GB 9—11, 134, 232, 243, 346, 353—8, 467—9, 523,
Worcester, GB 9—11, 134, 232,
Worcester, GB 9—11, 134, 232, 243, 346, 353—8, 467—9, 523, 524, 597, 599—606, 709, 796, 806, 807, 818—824, 885, 886, 917, 1027, 1681—3, 1713
Imitations 12, 2053
Wunsiedel, D 62, 63, 499
Würzburg, D 593, 1677, 1678

Yeiraku (Yamashiro province), J 1987—1990

Żary *see* Sorau
Zell-Harmersbach, D 1722, 1726—1730
Zofiówka *see* Charlottenbrunn
Zürich, CH 1719—1721
Zweibrücken, Gutenbrunn, D 1390, 1735
Zwickau, DDR 594, 1588, 1611

Ždanov *see* Tannawa
Žlutice *see* Lubenz

DATE DUE

PRINTED IN U.S.A.